THE WHEEL OF FORTUNE

THE WHEEL OF FORTUNE

MAHATMA GANDHI

Appreclation by

DWIJENDRANATH TAGORE

GYAN

Published by

GYAN

Gyan Publishing House
5, Ansari Road
Daryaganj, New Delhi-110002
Phone: 011-47034999, 9811692060
E-mail: books@gyanbooks.com

Distribution Network
gyanbooks.com
India, USA, Canada, UK, Australia, France

ISBN : 978-81-212-9146-0 (PB)
First Published, 1922

2nd Impression 2023

Printed at: Gyan Press, Delhi.

THE WHEEL OF FORTUNE
Author : MAHATMA GANDHI, Appreclation by : DWIJENDRANATH TAGORE

THE WHEEL OF FORTUNE

THE WHEEL OF FORTUNE

BY

MAHATMA GANDHI

Appreciation by

DWIJENDRANATH TAGORE

MADRAS

GANESH & CO.

1922

CONTENTS

APPENDICES

DAWN OF A NEW ERA

Many critics and some friends of Mahatma Gandhi have found fault with his desire to introduce simpler methods of spinning and weaving and to do away with much of the complicated machinery of Modern Civilisation. The reason why they object is that they fear such methods mean not progress towards a higher state but relapse into a primitive condition of civilisation or even of barbarism. His denunciation of the age of machinery and of the Industrial System has been criticised by many as the ravings of a visionary and of one who is merely an impracticable idealist. This is a strange criticism to come from those who give their allegiance to a form of civilisation or 'Culture' which has led to the unprecedented horrors of the late European War and the century-old disgraces of the Industrial System. Is this present modern civilisation so very desirable that we should wish it to continue in perpetuity? Every civilisation in the History of Man has reached a certain point after which there has been one possibility only for it and that was absolute relapse into semi-darkness in order to give place to a new and higher civilisation. The common starting point of all the civilisations is a kind of night-time. In order that the Babylonian (or Despotic) Civilisation might give way to the Roman (or Heroic), and the Roman give way to the Modern (or Intellectual) Civilisation, it was necessary for each in turn to sink completely into this common night-time. Without this entire destruction of the ancient structure, there would have been only a patchwork of the old, and not a harmonious building of the New. As Christ said: "Ye cannot put old wine into new bottles." The debris of the Past has to be cleared away in order to make way for the structure of the Future. Now with regard to Modern Civilisation, all the signs of the times show that it has failed lamentably and is gradually tottering to a dishonoured grave. Why make any attempts to prop up what Nature so evidently has decided to throw on the scrap-heap? Such attempts are contrary to the teaching of past history. But anything, which tends to reach the common roots of all civilisations, should be encouraged. In order that the spiritual civilisation of the Future may have a real chance of growing in an atmosphere congenial to it, Mahatma Gandhi's demonstration of the right path should be welcomed. His emphasis on simplicity of life and on the simplification of the machinery of living must be realised as a supremely essential condition of the coming of the new Era. In the civilisation of the Future, an Era of natural harmonious living will be inaugurated, and artificial, luxurious and pompous living will be entirely rooted out.

Simplicity of life being a condition of spiritual perfection, we may look forward to an Era of Civilisation in the Future, greatly superior to all the civilisations of the Past, if only we accept simplicity of life as the best method of living. The failure and decline of Western or Modern Civilisation need not alarm us; for the experience of History is full of similar declines of once powerful cultures. When Babylonian Civilisation had reached its height, it had to come down to what we may term the zero-point of all civilisation from which Roman Civilisation had made its start. But when Roman Civilisation had reached its zenith, it was much superior to the zenith Civilisation of Babylon, as the zenith Babylonian was superior to the zero-civilisation. And so also of full-fledged Modern Civilisation. We may say that until it returns to the common zero-point, there is no hope of a full and perfect development of a civilisation moulded by spiritual ideals.

Let critics of Mahatma Gandhi then look to History before they condemn him for trying to bring this much belauded Modern Civilisation down to the common starting point of all great civilisations. We are at the dawn of a New Era, and Mahatma Gandhi is the one leader who shows to us the right path. He at least is watering the roots, while all others who try to keep alive the Civilisation of the Western nations are like foolish gardeners who lavish water on the withering leaves of a dying tree and never think of watering its roots.

SWADESHI

THE WHEEL OF FORTUNE

BOYCOTT OF GOODS

vs.

NON-CO-OPERATION PROGRAMME

Mr. Kasturi Ranga Aiyangar was pleased to answer my argument in favour of the details of the first stage of non-co-operation that I had the honour of explaining at the great Madras Beach meeting. He expressed his dissent from all but the renunciation of titles. He suggested boycott of foreign goods in the place of the other items. Even at the risk of repeating arguments familiar to the readers of "Young India", I must deal with the question of boycott which has now received the imprimatur of so able a publicist as Mr. Kasturi Ranga Aiyangar.

In the first place, boycott of British goods has been conceived as a punishment and can have no place in non-co-operation which is conceived in a spirit of self-sacrifice and is a matter of sacred duty.

Secondly, any measure of punishment must be swift, certain and adequate for the effect intended to be produced. Resorted to by individuals, therefore, boycott is ineffectual, for, it can give no satisfaction unless it is productive of effect, whereas every act of non-co-operation is its own satisfaction.

Thirdly, boycott of British goods is thoroughly unpractical, for, it involves sacrifice of their millions by millionaires. It is in my opinion infinitely more difficult for a merchant to sacrifice his millions than for a lawyer to suspend his practice or for a title-holder to give up his title or for a parent to sacrifice, if need be, the literary instruction of his children. Add to this the important fact that merchants have only lately begun to interest themselves in politics. They are therefore yet timid and cautious. But the class, to which the first stage of non-co-operation is intended to appeal, is the political class which has devoted years to politics and is not mentally unprepared for communal sacrifice.

Boycott of British goods to be effective must be taken up by the whole country at once or not at all. It is like a siege. You can carry out a siege only when you have the requisite men and instruments of destruction. One man scratching a wall with his finger nails may hurt his fingers but will produce no effect upon the walls. One title-holder giving up his title has the supreme satisfaction of having washed his hands clean of the guilt of the donor and is unaffected by the refusal of his fellows to give up theirs. The motive of boycott being punitive lacks the inherent practicability of non-co-operation. The spirit of punishment is a sign of weakness. A strengthening of that spirit will retard the process of regeneration. The spirit of sacrifice is a determination to rid ourselves of our weakness. It is therefore an invigorating and purifying process and is therefore also calculated to do good both to us and to those who evoke the spirit of sacrifice in us. Above all, if India has a mission of her own, she will not fulfil it by copying the doubtful example of the West and making even her sacrifice materialistically utilitarian instead of offering a sacrifice spotless and pleasing even in the sight of God.

KHILAFAT AND SWADESHI

It was not without much misgiving that I consented to include Swadeshi as a plank in non-co-operation. But Maulana Hasrat Mohani by his sheer earnestness bore me down. I fear however that his reasons for including Swadeshi are different from mine. He is a protagonist of boycott of British goods, I cannot reconcile myself to the doctrine as I have explained elsewhere in this issue. But having failed to popularise boycott, Mohani Saheb has accepted Swadeshi as the lesser good. It is however necessary for me to explain how I have come to include Swadeshi in the programme of non-co-operation.

Non-co-operation is nothing but discipline in self-sacrifice. And I believe that a nation that is capable of limitless sacrifice is capable of rising to limitless heights. The purer the sacrifice the quicker the progress. Swadeshi offers every man, woman and child an occasion to make a beginning in self-sacrifice of a pure type. It therefore presents an opportunity for testing our capacity for sacrifice. It is the measure for gauging the depth of national feeling on the Khilafat wrong. Does the nation feel sufficiently to move it to go through even the preliminary process of sacrifice? Will the nation revise its taste for the Japanese silk, the Manchester calico or the French lace and find all its decoration out of hand-spun and hand-woven cloth, i.e., Khadi? If crores of people will refuse to wear or use foreign cloth and be satisfied with the simple cloth that we can produce in our homes, it will be proof of our organising ability, energy, co-operation and self-sacrifice that will enable us to secure all we need. It will be a striking demonstration of national solidarity.

Such a consummation cannot be achieved for the mere wish. It cannot be achieved by one man, no matter how capable and sincere he may be. It cannot be achieved by dotting India with Swadeshi stores. It can only be achieved by new production and judicious distribution. Production means lacs of women spinning in their own homes. This requires earnest men to be engaged in honestly distributing carded cotton and collecting yarn and paying for it. It means manufacture of thousands of spinning wheels. It means inducing the hereditary weavers to return to their noble calling and distributing home-spun yarn amongst them and setting their manufactures. It is thus only as an energising agent that I can think of Swadeshi as a plank in non-co-operation. But it is not to be despised in that capacity. And I hope that every worker for the cause, even if he can do nothing else, will have done something if he can advance Swadeshi first by increasing production and then distribution. He would be simply moving in a circle if he is satisfied with distributing cloth that is already being manufactured in India.

THE SECRET OF SWARAJ

THE Congress resolution has rightly emphasised the importance of Swadeshi and the amount of greater sacrifice by merchants.

India cannot be free so long as India voluntarily encourages or tolerates the economic drain which has been going on for the past century and a half. Boycott of foreign goods means no more and no less than boycott of foreign cloth. Foreign cloth constitutes the largest drain voluntarily permitted by us. It means sixty crores of rupees annually paid by us for piece-goods. If India could make a successful effort to stop that drain, she can gain Swaraj by that one act.

India was enslaved for satisfying the greed of the foreign cloth manufacturer. When the East India Company came in, we were able to manufacture all the cloth we needed, and more for export. By processes that need not be described here, India has become practically wholly dependent upon foreign manufacture for her clothing.

But we ought not to be dependent. India has the ability to manufacture all her cloth if her children will work for it. Fortunately India has yet enough weavers to supplement the out-turn of her mills. The mills do not and cannot immediately manufacture all the cloth we want. The reader may not know that, even at the present moment, the weavers weave more cloth than the mills. But the latter weave five crore yards of fine foreign counts, equal to forty crore yards of coarser counts. The way to carry out a successful boycott of foreign cloth is to increase the out-put of yarn. And this can only be done by hand-spinning.

To bring about such a boycott, it is necessary for our merchants to stop all foreign importation, and to sell out, even at a loss, all foreign cloth already stocked in India, preferably to foreign buyers. They must cease to speculate in cotton, and keep all the cotton required for home use. They must stop purchasing all foreign cotton.

The mill-owners should work their mills not for their profits but as a national trust and therefore cease to spin finer counts, and weave only for the home market.

The householder has to revise his or her ideas of fashion and, at least for the time being, suspend the use of fine garments which are not always worn to cover the body. He should train himself to see art and beauty in the spotlessly white *khaddar* and to appreciate its soft unevenness. The householder must learn to use cloth as a miser uses his horde.

And even when the householders have revised their tastes about dress, somebody will have to spin yarn for the weavers. This can only be done by every one spinning during spare hours either for love or money.

We are engaged in a spiritual war. We are not living in normal times. Normal activities are always suspended in abnormal times. And if we are out to gain

Swaraj in a year's time, it means that we must concentrate upon our goal to the exclusion of every thing else. I therefore venture to suggest to the students all over India to suspend their normal studies for one year and devote their time to the manufacture of yarn by hand-spinning. It will be their greatest act of service to the motherland, and their most natural contribution to the attainment of *Swaraj*. During the late war our rulers attempted to turn every factory into an arsenal for turning out bullets of lead. During this war of ours, I suggest every national school and college being turned into a factory for preparing cones of yarns for the nation. The students will lose nothing by the occupation: they will gain a kingdom here and hereafter. There is a famine of cloth in India. To assist in removing this dearth is surely an act of merit. If it is sinful to use foreign yarn, it is a virtue to manufacture more Swadeshi yarn in order to enable us to cope with the want that would be created by the disuse of foreign yarn.

The obvious question asked would be, if

it is so necessary to manufacture yarn, why not pay every poor person to do so? The answer is that hand spinning is not, and never was, a calling like weaving, carpentry, etc. Under the pre-British economy of India, spinning was an honourable and leisurely occupation for the women of India. It is difficult to revive the art among the women in the time at our disposal. But it is incredibly simple and easy for the school-goers to respond to the nation's call. Let no one decry the work as being derogatory to the dignity of man or students. It was an art confined to the women of India because the latter had more leisure. And being graceful, musical, and as it did not involve any great exertion, it had become the monopoly of women. But it is certainly as graceful for either sex as is music for instance. In hand-spinning is hidden the protection of women's virtue, the insurance against famine, and the cheapening of prices. In it is hidden the secret of *Swaraj*. The revival of hand spinning is the least penance we must do for the sin of our forefathers in having succumbed to the satanic influences of the foreign manufacturer.

The school-goers will restore hand-spinning to its respectable status. They will hasten the process of making *Khaddar* fashionable. For no mother, or father, worth the name will refuse to wear cloth made out of yarn spun by their children. And the scholars' practical recognition of art will compel the attention of the weavers of India. If we are to wean the Punjabi from the calling not of a soldier but of the murderer of innocent and free people of other lands, we must give back to him the occupation of weaving. The race of the peaceful Julahis of the Punjab is all but extinct. It is for the scholars of the Punjab to make it possible for the Punjabi weaver to return to his innocent calling.

I hope to show in a future issue how easy it is to introduce this change in the schools and how quickly, on these terms, we can nationalise our schools and colleges. Everywhere the students have asked me what new things I would introduce into our nationalised schools. I have invariably told them I would certainly introduce spinning. I feel, so much more clearly than ever before that during the transition period, we must devote exclusive attention to spinning and certain other things of immediate national use, so as to make up for past neglect. And the students will be better able and equipped to enter upon the new course of studies.

Do I want to put back the hand of the clock of progress? Do I want to replace the mills by hand-spinning and hand-weaving? Do I want to replace the railway by the country cart? Do I want to destroy machinery altogether? These questions have been asked by some journalists and public men. My answer is: I would not weep over the disappearance of machinery or consider it a calamity. But I have no design upon machinery as such. What I want to do at the present moment is to supplement the production of yarn and cloth through our mills, save the millions we send out of India, and distribute them in our cottages. This I cannot do unless and until the nation is prepared to devote its leisure hours to hand-spinning. To that end we must adopt the methods I have ventured to suggest for popularising spinning as a duty rather than as a means of ligmethods.

SWADESHI

In criticising my article entitled 'The Music of the Spinning Wheel!' the "Leader" the other day attributed to me the ideas that I have never entertained. And it is necessary for the purpose of understanding the true value of Swadeshi, to correct some of the current fallacies. The *Leader* considers that I am putting back the hands of the clock of progress by attempting to replace mill-made cloth and mill-spun yarn by hand-woven and hand-spun yarn. Now, I am making no such attempt at all. I have no quarrel with the mills. My views are incredibly simple. India requires nearly 13 yards of cloth per head per year. She produces, I believe, less than half the amount. India grows all the cotton she needs. She exports several million bales of cotton to Japan and Lancashire and receives much of it back in manufactured calico although she is capable of producing all the cloth and all the yarn necessary for supplying her wants by hand-weaving and hand-spinning. India needs to supplement her main occupation, agriculture, with some other employment. Hand-spinning is the only such employment for millions. It was the national employment a century ago. It is not true to say that economic pressure and modern machinery destroyed hand-spinning and hand-weaving. This great industry was destroyed or almost destroyed by extraordinary and immoral means adopted by the East India Company. This national industry is capable of being revived by exertion and a change in the national taste without damaging the mill industry. Increase of mills is no present remedy for supplying the deficiency. The difficulty can be easily supplied only by hand-spinning and hand-weaving. If this employment were revived, it would prevent sixty million rupees from being annually drained from the country and distribute the amount among lacs of poor women in their own cottages. I therefore consider Swadeshi as an automatic, though partial, solution of the problem of India's grinding poverty. It also constitutes a ready-made insurance policy in times of scarcity of rain.

But two things are needful to bring about the needed revival—to create a taste for Khaddar and to provide an organisation for the distribution of carded cotton and collection of yarn against payment.

In one year, by the silent labour of a few men, several thousand rupees have been distributed in Gujarat among several thousand poor women who are glad enough to earn a few pice per day to buy milk for their children, etc.

The argument does not apply to the sugar industry as the "Leader" has attempted. There is not sufficient cane grown in India to supply India's wants. Sugar was never a national and supplementary industry. Foreign sugar has not supplanted Indian sugar. India's wants of sugar have grown and she therefore imports more sugar. But this importation does not institute a drain in the sense in which importation of foreign cloth does. Production of more sugar means more scientific agriculture, more and better machinery for crushing and refining. The sugar industry therefore stands on a different platform. Swadeshi in sugar is desirable, Swadeshi in cloth is an urgent necessity.

The Swadeshi propaganda has been going on in a more or less organised manner now for the past eighteen months. Some of its results are surprising and gratifying. It has taken a fairly firm hold in the Punjab, Madras and the Bombay Presidency. Hand spinning and hand-weaving are steadily increasing in these parts. Several thousand rupees have been distributed in homes where women never did any work before. And if more work of this kind has not been done, it is due to want of workers.

This is however written more to note the mistakes of the past than to sum up the bright side. My observations lead me to the conclusion that whilst the inauguration of the three vows and Swadeshi stores have greatly stimulated the Swadeshi spirit, it is no longer possible to advocate the taking of any of the three vows or the opening of new Swadeshi stores for the sale of mill-made cloth. The result of the propaganda has been to send up the prices of yarn and cloth rather than increase production. It is clear that the purpose of Swadeshi is not served until the quantity of yarn and cloth produced is increased. The gain therefore is merely moral and not material. The people have begun to perceive the desirability of wearing only Swadeshi cloth if the real interest of the country is to be advanced.

But it is clear that we must take practical steps for meeting the growing demand for Swadeshi cloth. One way, no doubt, is to increase the mills. But it is obvious that capitalists do not need popular encouragement. They know that India needs much more cloth than is manufactured by our mills. But mills do not spring up like mushrooms. It is a matter of getting machinery from outside, let alone the difficulty of getting labour. And after all, India cannot become truly and economically independent so long as she must rely on the supply of machinery from outside for the manufacture of her cloth.

The cleanest and the most popular form of Swadeshi, therefore, is to stimulate hand-spinning and hand-weaving and to arrange for a judicious distribution of yarn and cloth so manufactured. With a little talent and a little industry this thing is easy. Even as each home cooks its own food without difficulty, so may each home weave its own yarn. And just as in spite of every home having its own kitchen, restaurants continue to flourish, so will mills continue to supply our additional wants. But even as because of our private kitchens we would not starve if every restaurant was through some accident closed, so would we, by reason of domestic spinning, not have to be naked even if every mill, by a blockade from the west, had to stop work. Not long ago, we knew this secret of our own economic independence and it is possible for us to regain that independence by a little effort, a little organising agency and a little sacrifice.

The officials are so ignorant and obstinate, that they will not take the only effective course for avoiding the feared 'disorders and looting,' *viz.* making common cause with the public and stimulating production. Instead of recognising the agitation against foreign cloth as desirable and necessary, they regard it as an evil to be put down. And then it is complained, that I call a system which seeks to thwart healthy public agitation, satanic. Why should there be any dearth of indigenous cloth? Is there not enough cotton in India? Are there not enough men and women who can spin and weave? Is it not possible to manufacture all the required number of wheels in a few days? Why should not each home manufacture its own cloth, even as it cooks its own food? Is it not enough in times of famine to distribute uncooked grain among the famine-striken? Why should it not be enough to distribute raw cotton among those who need clothing? Why this hypocritical or false alarm about the dearth of cloth, when it is possible in India to manufacture enough for India's needs in a month even without the aid of the mills? The people have been purposely or ignorantly kept in the dark hitherto. They have been wrongly taught to believe, that all the cloth needed cannot be manufactured in India's homes as of yore. They have been figuratively amputated and then made to rely upon foreign or mill-made cloth. I wish the people concerned will give the only dignified answer possible to these circulars. They will forthwith burn or send out all their foreign cloth, and courageously make up their minds to spin and weave for their own requirements. It is incredibly easy for every one who is not an idler. *Y. I.—18th Aug. 1920.*

SWADESHI IN THE PUNJAB

THE Joint Secretaries of the Bharat Stri Maha Mandal, Punjab Branch, send a report of the Swadeshi activities of Shrimati Saraladevi Chaudhrani ever since her return to Lahore from Bombay. Miss Roy and Mrs. Roshandal, the Secretaries, state that meetings of women were held respectively on the 23rd, 24th and 25th June at three different places in Lahore. All the meetings were attended by hundreds of women who were deeply interested in what Shrimati Saraladevi had to say. The burden of her discourses was India's deep poverty. She traced the causes and proved that our poverty was primarily due to the abandonment of Swadeshi by the people. The remedy therefore lay in reverting to Swadeshi.

Saraladevi herself writes to say that her Khaddar Sari impressed her audiences more than her speeches, and her songs came next, her speeches last. The good ladies of Lahore flocked round her and left her coarse but beautifully white Sari and admired it. Some took pity on her that she who only the other day was dressed in costly thin silk Saris now decked herself in hand-woven Swadeshi Khaddar. Saraladevi wanted no pity and retorted that their thin foreign scarves lay heavier on their shoulders with the weight of their helpless dependence on foreign manufacture whereas her coarse Khaddar lay light as a feather on her body with the joy of the knowledge that she was free because she wore garments in the manufacture of which her sisters and her brothers had laboured. This statement so pleased her audience that most of the women present resolved to discard foreign clothes. Saraladevi has now been charged by these ladies to open a shop where they could buy Swadeshi goods. She has since addressed more audiences. She spoke at the District Conference at Sialkot and to a meeting exclusively devoted to ladies numbering over one thousand. I hope that the men of Punjab will help Saraladevi in her self-imposed mission. They may harness her talents and her willingness in founding Swadeshi Sabha and organasing Swadeshi propaganda on a sound basis. Both men and money are needed to make the work a success.

Swadeshi is more than reforms. There is much waste over reforms. There is none in Swadeshi. Every yard of yarn spun is so much labour well spent and so much wealth added to the national treasury. Every drop counts Swadeshi spells first production and then distribution. Distribution without production means the raising of prices without any corresponding benefit. For to-day demand exceeds the supply. If we will not manufacture more cloth, more foreign imports must continue a painful and sinful necessity.

Punjab has a great opportunity. Punjab grows splendid cotton. The art of spinning has not yet died out. Almost every Punjabi woman knows it. This sacred haunt of the Rishis of old has thousands of weavers.

Only the leaders need to have faith in their women and themselves. When Saraladevi wrote to me that she might want goods from Bombay, I felt hurt. The Punjab has all the time and all the labour and the material necessary for producing her own cloth. She has brave merchants. She has more than enough capital. She has brains. Has she the will? She can organise her own Swadeshi in less than a year, if the leaders will work at this great cause. It is playing with Swadeshi for the Punjab to have to import cloth from Bombay.

The Punjab has to right herself by putting her Swadeshi on a proper basis and by ridding herself of Messrs. Bosworth Smith and Company. She will then be both economically and politically sound. Geographically she stands at the top. She led the way in the older times. Will she again do so? Her men are virile to look at. Have they virility enough to secure without a moment's delay purity of administration? I have not strayed from Swadeshi to politics. My Swadeshi spirit makes me impatient of garments that denude India of her wealth and equally impatient of the Smiths, the O'Briens, the Shri Rams and the Maliks who denude her of her self-respect and insolently touch women's veils with their sticks, chain innocent men as if they were beasts, or shoot them from armoured cars or otherwise terrorise people into subjection.

Y. I.—7th July 1920.

SWADESHI STORES

IN a previous issue I endeavoured to show how stores for the sake of selling mill-manufactures did not advance Swadeshi in any way whatsoever but on the contrary, tended to send up the price of cloth. I propose to show in this article how with a small capital, it is possible to advance true Swadeshi and earn a modest livelihood.

Suppose that there is a family consisting of husband, wife and two children one of whom is ten years old and the other five. If they have a capital of Rs. 500 they can manage a Khaddar Bhandar in a small way. They can hire, say in a place with a population of 20,000 inhabitants a shop with dwelling rooms for Rs. 10 per month. If they sell the whole of the stock at 10 p.c. profit they can have Rs. 50 per month. They have no servants. The wife and the children in their spare time would be expected to help in keeping the shop tidy and looking after it when the husband is out. The wife and children can also devote their spare time to spinning.

In the initial stages the Khaddar may not sell at the shop. In that case the husband is expected to hawk the Khaddar from door to door and popularise it. He will soon find a custom for it.

The reader must not be surprised at my suggesting 10 p.c. profits. The Khaddar Bhandars are not designed for the poorest. The use of Khaddar saves at least half the cost not necessarily because the Khaddar is more durable (though that it certainly is) but because its use revolutionises our tastes. I know what saving of money its use has meant to me. Those, who buy Khaddar from patroitic motives merely, can easily afford to pay 10 p.c. profits on Khaddar. Lastly the popularising of Khaddar means much care, devotion and labour. And the owner of a Khaddar Bhandar does not buy it at a wholesale shop but he must wander to get the best

Khaddar, he must meet the local weavers and induce them to weave hand spun yarn. He must stimulate in his own district hand spinning among its women. He must come in touch with the carders and get them to card cotton. All this means intelligence, organisation and great ability. A man who can exhibit these qualities has a right to take 10 p.c. profits. And a Swadeshi Bhandar conducted on these lines becomes a true centre of Swadeshi activity. I commend my remarks to the attention of the managers of Swadeshi stores that are already in existence. They may not revolutionise their method at once but I have no doubt that they will advance Swadeshi only to the extent that they sell Khaddar. *Y. I.—7th July, 1920.*

INDIAN ECONOMICS

A friend has placed in my hands a bulletin on Indian Piece Goods Trade prepared by Mr. A. C. Coubrough C. B. E. by order of the Government of India. It contains the following prefatory note: 'The Government of India desire it to be understood that the statements made and the views expressed in this buelletin are those of the author himself.' If so, why has the Government of India burdened the tax-payer with the expense of such bulletins? The one before me is 16th in the series. Do they publish both the sides of the question ?

The bulletin under review is intended to be an answer to the Swadeshi movement. It is an elaborate note containing a number of charts showing the condition of imports and home manufacture of piece goods including hand-woven. But it does not assist the reader in studying the movement.

The painstaking author has bestowed no pains upon a study of the present movement or its scope. That the Government of India treats the greatest constructive and co-operative movement in the country with supreme contempt and devotes people's money to a vain refutation instead of a sympathetic study and treatment is perhaps the best condemnation that can be pronounced upon the system under which it is carried.

The author's argument is:

(1) The movement if successful will act not as a protective but a prohibitive tariff.

(2) This must result in merely enriching the Indian capitalist and punishing the consumer.

(3) The imports are non-competitive in that the bulk of the kind of piece goods imported are not manufactured in India.

(4) The result of boycotting such piece goods must be high prices without corresponding benefit.

(5) The boycott therefore being aginst the law of supply and demand and against the consumer must fail in the end.

(6) The destruction of hand spinning which I have deplored is due to natural causes, *viz.* the invention of time-saving appliances and was therefore inevitable.

(7) The Indian farmer is responsible for his own ruin in that he has indolently neglected cotton culture which was once so good.

(8) The best service I can render is therefore to induce the agriculturist to improve the quality of cotton.

(9) The author concludes, 'If instead of filling homes with useless *Charkhas* he were to start a propaganda for the more intensive cultivation of cotton and particularly for the production of longer staple cotton, his influence would be felt not only at the present day but for many generations to come.'

The reader will thus see, that what I regard as the supreme necessity for the economical salvation of India, the author considers to be rank folly. There is therefore no meeting ground here. And in spite of the prefatory note of the Government of India reproduced by me, the another does represent the Government attitude. I have invited them and the co-operators definitely to make common cause with the people in this movement at any rate. They may not mind its political implications because they do not believe in them. And surely they need not feel sorry if contrary to their expectation, the rise of the *Charkha* results in an increase in the political power of the people. Instead of waging war against *Khadi*, they might have popularised its use and disarmed the terrible suspicion they labour under of wishing to benefit the foreign manufacturer at the expense of the Indian cultivator. My invitation is open for all time. I prophesy that whatever happens to the other parts of the national programme, Swadeshi in its present shape will bide for ever and must if India's pauperism is to be banished.

Even though I am a layman, I make bold to say that the so-called laws laid down in books on economics are not immutable like the laws of Medes and Persians, nor are they universal. The economics of England are different from those of Germany. Germany enriched herself by bounty-fed beet sugar. England enriched herself by exploiting foreign markets. What was possible for a compact area is not possible for an area 1,900 miles long and 1,500 broad. The economics of a nation are determined by its climatic, geological and temperamental conditions. The Indian conditions are different from the English in all these essentials. What is meat for England is in many cases poison for India. Beef tea in the English climate may be good, it is poison for the hot climate of religious India. Fiery whisky in the north of the British Isles may be a necessity, it renders an Indian unfit for work or society. Fur-coats in Scotland are indispensable, they will be an intolerable burden in India. Free trade for a country which has become industrial, whose population can and does live in cities, whose people do not mind preying upon other nations and therefore sustain the biggest navy to protect their unnatural commerce, may be economically sound (though as the reader perceives, I question its morality). Free trade for India has proved her curse and held her in bondage.

And now for Mr. Coubrough's propositions.

(1) The movement is intended to serve the purpose of a voluntary prohibitive tariff.

(2) But it is so conceived as neither unduly to benefit the capitalist nor to injure the consumer. During the very brief transition stage the prices of home manufactures may be, as they are, inflated. But the rise can only be temporary as the vast majority of consumers must become their own manufacturers. This cottage manufacture of yarn and cloth cannot be expensive even as domestic cookery is not expensive and cannot be replaced by hotel cookery. Over twenty-five crores of the population will be doing their own hand-spinning and having yarn thus manufactured woven in neighbouring localities. This population is rooted to the soil and has at least four months in the year to remain idle.

If they spin during those hours and have the yarn woven and wear it, no mill-made cloth can compete with their *Khadi*. The cloth thus manufactured will be the cheapest possible for them. If the rest of the population did not take part in the process, it could easily be supplied out of the surplus manufactured by the twenty-five crores.

(3) It is true that non-competitive imports are larger than those that compete with the manufactures of Indian mills. In the scheme proposed by me the question does not arise, because the central idea is not so much to carry on a commercial war against foreign countries as to utlise the idle hours of the nation and thus by natural processes to help it to get rid of her growing pauperism.

(4) I have already shown that the result of boycott cannot in the end be a rise in the price of cloth.

(5) The proposed boycott is not against the law of supply and demand, because it does away with the law by manufacturing enough for the supply. The movement does require a change of taste on the part of those who have adopted finer variety

and who patronise fantastic combinations of colours and designs.

(6) I have shown in these pages, that the destruction of hand-spinning was designed and carried out in a most inhuman manner by the agents of the East India Company. No amount of appliances would ever have displaced this national art and industry but for this artificial and systematically cruel manner of carrying out the destruction.

(7) I am unable to hold the Indian farmer responsible for the deterioration in cotton culture. The whole incentive was taken away when hand-spinning was destroyed. The State never cared for the cultivator.

(8) My activity, I am proud to think, has already turned the cultivator's attention to the improvement of cotton. The artistic sense of the nation will insist on fine counts for which long staple is a necessity. Cotton culture by itself cannot solve the problem of India's poverty. For it will still leave the question of enforced idleness untouched.

(9) I therefore claim for the *Charkha* the honour of being able to solve the problem of economic distress in a most natural, simple, unexpensive and business-like manner. The *Charkha*, therefore, is not only not useless as the writer ignorantly suggests, but it is a useful and indispensable article for every home. It is the symbol of the nation's prosperity and therefore, freedom. It is a symbol not of commercial war but of commercial peace. It bears not a message of ill-will towards the nations of the earth but of good-will and self-help. It will not need the protection of a navy threatening a world's peace and exploiting its resources, but it needs the religious determination of millions to spin their yarn in their own homes as to-day they cook their food in their own homes. I may deserve the curses of posterity for many mistakes of omission and commission but I am confident of earning its blessings for suggesting a revival of the *Charkha*. I stake my all on it. For every revolution of the wheel spins peace, good-will and love. And with all

that, inasmuch as the loss of it brought about India's slavery, its voluntary revival with all its implications must mean India's freedom. *Y. I.—8th Dec. 1921.*

HOW TO BOYCOTT FOREIGN CLOTH

IT is needness to say at this time of the day, that the proposed boycott of foreign cloth is not a vindictive measure, but is as necessary for national existence as breath is for life. The quicker, therefore, it can be brought about, the better for the country. Without it, Swaraj cannot be established or retained after establishment. It is of the highest importance to know how it can be brought about even before the first day of August next.

To arrive at the boycott quickly, it is necessary (1) for the mill-owners to regulate their profits and to manufacture principally for the Indian market, (2) for importers to cease to buy foreign goods. A beginning has already been made by three principal merchants, (3) for the consumers to refuse to buy any foreign cloth and to buy *Khadi* wherever possible, (4) for the consumers to wear only *Khadi* cloth, mill cloth being retained for the poor who do not know the distinction between Swadeshi and Pardeshi, (5) for the consumers to use, till Swaraj is established and *Khadi* manufacture increased, *Khadi* just enough for covering the body, (6) for the consumers to destroy Pardeshi cloth, as they would destroy intoxicating liquors on taking the vow of abstinence, or to sell it for use abroad, or to wear it out for all dirty work or during private hours.

It is to be hoped that all the parties referred to in the foregoing clauses will respond well and simultaneously. But in the end success depends upon the persistent determination of the consumer. He has simply to decline to wear the badge of his slavery.

Abusing the khaddar—A friend draws attention to the fact that many who have adopted the *khaddar* costume are using it as a passport for arrogance, insolence, and, what is worse, fraud. He says that they have neither the spirit of non-co-operation in them nor the spirit of truth. They simply use the *khaddar* dress as a cloak for their deceit. All this is likely, especially during the transition stage, i.e., whilst *khaddar* is beginning to become fashionable. I would only suggest to my correspondent that such abuse of *khaddar* must not even unconsciously be allowed to be used as an argument against its use. Its use to-day is obligatory on those who believe that there is not sufficient Indian mill-made cloth to supply the wants of the nation, that the wants must be supplied in the quickest way possible by increasing home manufacture, and that such manufacture is possible only by making home-spinning universal. The use of *khaddar* represents nothing more than a most practical recognition of the greatest economic necessity of the country. Even a scoundrel may recognise this necessity, and has therefore a perfect right to wear it. And if a Government spy wore it to deceive people, I would welcome his use of *khaddar* as so much economic gain to the country. Only I would not give the wearer of the *khaddar* more than his due

And I would therefore not ascribe to him any piety or special virtue. It follows, therefore, that co-operationists or government servants may wear *khaddar* without incurring the danger of being mistaken for non-co-operationists. We may no more shun *khaddar*, than a devout church-goer may renounce his church because bad characters go to it for duping gullible people. I recall the name of an M. P. who successfully cloaked many of his vices by pretending to be a staunch temperance man. Not very long ago a bold and unscrupulous speculator found entry into most respectable circles by becoming a temperance advocate. Well has a poet said that 'hypocricy is an ode to virtue.'

Some 'ifs'—If you are a *weaver* feeling for the country, the Khilafat and the Punjab,

(1) You should weave only hand-spun yarn, and charge so as to give you a living. You should overcome all the difficulties of sizing and adjusting your loom to the requirements of coarse yarn.

(2) If you cannot possibly tackle hand-

spun yarn for warp, you must use Indian mill-spun yarn for it and use hand-spun for woof.

(3) Where even the second alternative is not possible, you should use mill-spun yarn for both warp and woof.

But you should henceforth cease to use any foreign yarn, whether it is silk or cotton.

If you are a *Congress official or worker*, you should get hold of the weavers within your jurisdiction, and place the foregoing propositions before them for acceptance and help them to the best of your ability.

If you are a *buyer*, insist upon the first class of cloth, but if you have not the sense or the courage to do so, take up the second or the third, but on no account purchase foreign cloth or cloth woven in India but made of foreign yarn.

If you are a *householder*,

(1) You should make a fixed determination henceforth not to buy any foreign cloth.

(2) You should interview the weaver in your neighbourhood, and get him to weave

for you enough *khadi* out of home-spun and failing that to weave out of Indian mill-spun yarn.

(3) You should deliver to the Congress Committee all your foreign cloth for destruction or sending to Smyrna or elsewhere outside India.

(4) If you have not the courage to give up your foreign cloth, you may wear it out at home for all dirty work, but never go out in foreign cloth.

(5) If you have any leisure, you should devote it to learning the art of spinning even, properly-twisted yarn for the sake of the nation.

If you are a *schoolboy or schoolgirl*, you should consider it a sin to receive literary training, before you have spun, carded or woven for the nation for at least four hours per day till the establishment of Swaraj. *Y. I.—6th July 1921.*

SPINNING

THE MUSIC OF THE SPINNING WHEEL

SLOWLY but surely the music of perhaps the most ancient machine of India is once more permeating society. Pandit Malaviyaji has stated that he is not going to be satisfied until the Ranis and the Maharanis of India spin yarn for the nation, and the Ranas and the Maharanas sit behind the handlooms and weave cloth for the nation. They have the example of Aurangzeb who made his own caps. A greater emperor—Kabir—was himself a weaver and has immortalised the art in his poems. The queens of Europe, before Europe was caught in Satan's trap, spun yarn and considered it a noble calling. The very words, spinster and wife, prove the ancient dignity of the art of spinning and weaving. 'When Adam delved and Eve span, who was then a gentleman,' also reminds one of the same fact. Well may Panditji hope to persuade the royalty of India to return to the ancient calling of this sacred land of ours. Not on the clatter of arms depends the revival of her prosperity and true independence. It depends most largely upon re-introduction, in every home, of the music of the spinning wheel. It gives sweeter music and is more profitable than the execrable harmonium, concertina and the accordian.

Whilst Panditji is endeavouring in his inimitably suave manner to persuade the Indian royalty to take up the spinning wheel, Shrimati Sarala Devi Choudhrani, who is herself a member of the Indian nobility, has learnt the art and has thrown herself heart and soul into the movement. From all the accounts received from her and others, Swadeshi has become a passion with her. She says she feels uncomfortable in her muslin saris and is content to wear her *khaddar* saris even in the hot weather. Her *khaddar* saris continue to preach true Swadeshi more eloquently than her tongue. She has spoken to audiences in Amritsar, Ludhiana and elsewhere and has succeeded in enlisting the services, for her Spinning Committee at Amritsar, of Mrs. Ratanchand and Bugga Chowdhry and the famous Ratan Devi who during the frightful night of the 13th April despite the Curfew Order of General Dyer sat, all alone in the midst of the hundreds of the dead and dying, with her dead husband's cold head in her lap. I venture to tender my congratulations to these ladies. May they find solace in the music of the spinning wheel and in the thought that they are doing national work. I hope that the other ladies of Amritsar will help Sarala Devi in her efforts and that the men of Amritsar will realise their own duty in the matter.

In Bombay the readers are aware that ladies of noted families have already taken up spinning. Their ranks have been joined by Dr. Mrs. Manekbai Bahudarji who has already learnt the art and who is now trying to introduce it in the Sevasadan. Her Highness the Begum Saheba of Janjira and her sister Mrs. Atia Begum Rahiman, have also undertaken to learn the art. I trust that these good ladies will, having learnt spinning, religiously contribute to the nation their daily quota of yarn.

I know that there are friends who laugh at this attempt to revive this great art. They remind me that in these days of mills, sewing machines or typewriters, only a lunatic can hope to succeed in reviving the rusticated spinning wheel. These friends forget that the needle has not yet given place to the sewing machine nor has the hand lost its cunning in spite of the typewriter. There is not the slightest reason why the spinning wheel may not co-exist with the spinning mill even as the domestic kitchen co-exists with the hotels. Indeed typewriters and sewing machines may go, but the needle and the reed pen will survive. The mills may suffer destruction. The spinning wheel is a national necessity. I would ask sceptics to go to the many poor homes where the spinning wheel is again supplementing their slender resources and ask the inmates whether the spinning wheel has not brought joy to their homes.

Thank God, the reward issued by Mr. Rewashanker Jagjiwan bids fare to bear fruit. In a short time India will possess a renovated spinning wheel—a wonderful invention of a patient Deccan artisan. It is made out of simple materials. There is no great complication about it. It will be cheap and capable of being easily mended. It will give more yarn than the ordinary wheel and is capable of being worked by a five years old boy or girl. But whether the new machine proves what it claims to be or it does not, I feel convinced that the revival of hand-spinning and hand-weaving will make the largest contribution to the economic and the moral regeneration of India. The millions must have a simple industry to supplement agriculture. Spinning was the cottage industry years ago and if the millions are to be saved from starvation, they must be enabled to reintroduce spinning in their homes, and every village must repossess its own weaver. *Y. I.—21st July 1920.*

"HANDLOOMS OR POWERMILLS?"

WHENEVER an attempt has been made, as it is being made to-day, to encourage the use and production of hand-spun and hand-woven cloth, many have looked askance whether it is intended in this age of mechanical industrialism to supplant the latter by medieval handlooms. The issue is placed between the hand power and the power mill. A correspondent of the *Janmabhumi* falls into this common error. Apparently agitated at the idea of reviving the home industries, he exclaims, "The real question for consideration with us or with any people to-day is not whether the handloom will or will not be able to hold its own against the power loom, or whether it cannot feed millions of families or clothe millions more in home-made dress; but which will contribute to the economic and political power of a nation or country, whether it is the handloom or the power-mill? Handicrafts or machine industries—that is the real issue."

It is not quite clear from the above what the notions of the correspondent are about the economic and political power of this country. We cannot imagine him to seriously believe—though his argument runs as if he does—that that power can be achieved without feeding and clothing the millions of our half-starving and half-naked men, women and children. The political and economic power of a nation depends even in this "age of mechanical industrialism," not on its powerful machines but on its powerful men. Germany was equipped with the best and most powerful and modern machinery, but it failed because at the last moment the power of its nation failed. We want to organise our national power. This can be done not by adopting the best methods of production only but by the best method of *both* the production and the distribution. Production that is the manufacture of cloth in this particular instance can be brought about in two ways;

(1) by establishing new mills and increasing the output or producing capacity of each mill and (2) by increasing the number of hand-looms and improving them. All these activities can go together. The notion of a competition between the hand-loom and the power mill has been shown by such an eminent economist as Prof. Radha Kamal Mukerjea to be "altogether wrong." Says Mr. Mukerjea in his *Foundations of Indian Economics*:

"The hand-loom does not compete with the mill, it supplements it in the following way:

(1) It produces special kinds of goods which cannot be woven in the mills.

(2) It utilizes yarn below and above certain counts which cannot at present be used on the power-mill.

(3) It will consume the surplus stock of Indian spinning mills which need not then be sent out of the country.

(4) Being mainly a village-industry, it supplies the local demand, at the same time gives employment to small capitalists, weavers and other village workmen and

(5) lastly it will supply the long-felt want of, and honest field of, work and livelihood for educated Indians."

But even this is not all that can be said in favour of hand-loom industry. Mill industry no doubt can be a powerful aid to the promotion of Swadeshi. But apart from the bitter struggle, strife and demoralisation of the capitalist and the workman (as explained by the eminent scholar, administrator and economist, the late Mr. Romesh Chundra Dutt) it has led to, the question is: Can it solve the problem which pure Swadeshi is designed and sought to do and which arises only because of its abandonment? Every writer of note on the industries of India, whatever his ideas and conclusions about the future of Indian Industrialism may be, has shown that there was a time and that was even till the Early British Rule in India—where spinning and weaving, only next to agriculture, were the great national industries of India, when all the cotton was spun by hand and every portion of the work was done by the farming population which augmented its resources by spinning and weaving. Mr. Dutt has given extracts from the statistical observations of Dr. Francis Buchanan's economic enquiries in Southern and Northern India, conducted between 1798 and 1814. They show how many hundreds of thousands of our men, women and children worked on this industry—mostly in their leisure time—each day and earned crores of rupees annually.

How our home-industries came to the sad plight they are in to-day is an open secret, admitted by all authorities and need not be repeated here. Suffice it to say that the problem to-day is not to bring about that political and economic re-organisation of our country, which disturbs the West to-day—an organisation which has led to the breaking up of the society by ceaseless struggles, bitterness and rupture between Capital and Labour. We want to work out the real political and economic regeneration of the country by Swadeshi. And the problem of the Swadeshi is the problem of 80 per cent. of our population who spend more than six months of the year in enforced idleness, eking, throughout the year, a miserable, half-starving and half-naked existence. We must find out suitable work for them during their idle hours. We must make them a real asset and power to the nation. Pure Swadeshi alone can do it. *Y. I.—28th July 1920.*

HAND-SPINNING AND HAND-WEAVING

SOME people spurn the idea of making in this age of mechanism hand-spinning and hand-weaving a national industry, but they forget there are millions of their countrymen in this age who, for want of suitable occupation, are eking out a most miserable existence, and thousands who die of starvation and underfeeding every year, whereas only a hundred years ago hand-spinning and hand-weaving proved an insurance against a pauper's death. The extent to which relief was provided by this industry is recorded by Mr. Dutt in his "History of India: Victorian age" from the investigations conducted by Dr. Buchanan for seven years, 1813-1820. Dr. Buchanan travelled throughout of the whole country. And his observations and statistics convinced him that next to agriculture, hand-spinning and hand-weaving were the great national industries. We makê no apology for giving some of the facts and figures collected by Dr. Buchanan :

In the districts of Patna and Behar with a population of 3,364,420 souls, the number of spinners was 330,426. "By far the greater part of these," observed Dr. Buchanan, "spin only a few hours in the afternoon, and upon the average estimate the whole value of the thread that each spins in a year is worth Rs. 7-2-8 giving a total annual income of Rs. 23,67,277 and by a similar calculation the raw material at the retail price will amount to Rs. 12,86,272, leaving a profit of Rs. 10,81,005 for the spinners or Rs. 3-4-0 per spinner..."

In the district of Shahbad, spinning was the chief industry. 159,500 women were employed in spinning and spun yarn to the value of Rs. 12,50,000 a year. Deducting the value of cotton each woman had some thing left to her to add to the income of the family to which she belonged.

In the Bhagalpur district (*with a*

population of 2,019,900) where all castes were permitted to spin, 160,000 women spent a part of their time in spinning and each made an annual income of Rs. 4½ after deducting the cost of cotton. This was added to the family income. In the Gorakhpur district (population 1,385,495) 175,600 women found employment in spinning and made an annual income of Rs. 2½ per head. In the Dinjapur district (with a population of 300,000) cotton-spinning which was the principal manufacture occupied the leisure hours 'of all women of higher rank and of the greater part of the farmers' wives.' Three rupees was the annual income each woman made by spinning in her afternoon hours.

In the Purniya district (population 2,904,380) all castes considered spinning honourable and a very large population of women of the district did some spinning in their leisure hours.

In eastern Mysore women of all castes except Brahmans bought cotton and wool at weekly markets, spun at home, and sold the thread to weavers. Men and women thus found a profitable occupation. In Coimbatore, the wives of all the low class cultivators were great spinners.

The statistics of weavers show that they also were as numerous as the spinners. In the Patna city and Behar district, the total number of looms employed in the manufacture of chaddars and table cloths was 750, and the value of the annual manufactures was Rs. 5,40,000 leaving a profit of Rs. 81,400, deducting the value of thread. This gave a profit of Rs. 108 for each loom worked by three persons or an income of Rs. 36 a year for each person. But the greater part of the cloth-weavers made coarse cloth for country use to the value of Rs. 24,386,621 after deducting the cost of thread. This gave a profit of Rs. 28 for each loom.

In Shahabad weavers worked in cotton only. 7,025 houses of weavers worked in cotton and had 7,950 looms. Each loom made an annual income of Rs. 20¾ a year and each loom required the labour of a man and his wife as well as one boy or girl. But as a family could not be supported for less than Rs. 48 a year, Dr. Buchanan suspected that the income of each loom given above was understated.

In the Bhagalpur district some worked in silk alone. A great many near the town made Tasar fabrics of silk and cotton intermixed; 3,275 looms were so employed that the annual profit of each weaver employed in the mixed silk and cotton industry was calculated to be Rs. 46 besides what the woman made.

For the weaving of cotton-cloth, there were 7,279 looms. Each loom yielded a profit of Rs. 20 a year. But by another calculation, Dr. Buchanan estimated it to be Rs. 32 a year.

In the Gorakhpur district there were 5,434 families of weavers possessing 6,174 looms and each loom brought an income of Rs. 23½. Dr. Buchanan thought this was too low an estimate and believed that each loom brought an income of Rs. 88 in the year.

In the Dungarpur district "Maldai" cloth was manufactured. It consisted of silk warp and cotton woof. 4,000 looms were employed in this work and it was said that each loom made Rs. 20 worth of cloth in a month, which Dr. Buchanan considered too high an estimate. About 800 looms were employed in making larger pieces in the form of Elachis.

In the Purniya district weavers were numerous......In Eastern Mysore cotton-weavers made cloth for home-use as silk weavers produced a strong rich fabric. Workmen who made cloth with silk borders earned As. 6 a day and those who made silk cloth earned As. 4

Thus we see that crores of rupees were earned by these spinners and weavers by following their noble and honest calling. The decentralisation of the industry—every village, town and district having always at its command as much supply as it needed-automatically facilitated its distribution and saved the consumer from Railway Excise and all sorts of tariffs and middlemen's profits that he is a victim to-day. If we cannot return to these days-though there is no reason, except our own bias and doubt why we should not—can we not at least so organise our industries as to do away without much delay with the foreign cloth with which our markets are being dumped to-day? *Y. I.—15th Sep. 1920.*

HAND-SPINNING AGAIN

The Servant of India has a fling too at spinning and that is based as I shall presently show on ignorance of the facts. Spinning does protect a woman's virtue, because it enables women, who are to-day working on public roads and are often in danger of having their modesty outraged, to protect themselves, and I know no other occupation that lacs of women can follow save spinning. Let me inform the jesting writer that several women have already returned to the sanctity of their homes and taken to spinning which they say is the one occupation which means so much *barkat* (blessing). I claim for it the properties of a musical instrument, for whilst a hungry and a naked woman will refuse to dance to the accompaniment of a piano, I have seen women beaming with joy to see the spinning wheel work, for they know that they can through that rustic instrument both feed and clothe themselves.

Yes, it does solve the problem of India's chronic poverty and is an insurance against famine. The writer of the jests may not know the scandals that I know about irrigation and relief works. These works are largely a fraud. But if my wise counsellors will devote themselves to introducing the wheel in every home, I promise that the wheel will be an almost complete protection against famine. It is idle to cite Austria. I admit the poverty and limitations of my humanity. I can only think of India's *Kamadhenu,* and the spinning wheel is that for India. For India had the spinning wheel in every home before the advent of the East India Company. India being a cotton growing country, it must be considered a crime to import a single yard of yarn from outside. The figures quoted by the writer are irrelevant.

The fact is that in spite of the manufacture of 62·7 crores pounds of yarn in 1917-18

India imported several crore yards of foreign yarn which were woven by the mills as well as the weavers. The writer does not also seem to know that more cloth is to-day woven by our weavers than by mills, but the bulk of it is foreign yarn and therefore our weavers are supporting foreign spinners. I would not mind it much if we were doing something else instead. When spinning was almost compulsorily stopped nothing replaced it save slavery and idleness. Our mills cannot to-day spin enough for our wants, and if they did, they will not keep down prices unless they were compelled. They are frankly money-makers and will not therefore regulate prices according to the needs of the nations. Hand-spinning is therefore designed to put millions of rupees in the hands of poor villagers. Every agricultural country requires a supplementary industry to enable the peasants to utilise the spare hours. Such industry for India has always been spinning. Is it such a visionary ideal—an attempt to revive an ancient occupation whose destruction has brought on slavery, pauperism and disappearance of the inimitable artistic talents which was once all expressed in the wonderful fabric of India and which was the envy of the world?

And now a few figures. One boy could, if he worked say four hours daily, spin ¼ lb. of yarn. 64,000 students would, therefore, spin 16,000 lbs. per day, and therefore feed 8,000 weavers if a weaver wove two lbs. of hand-spun yarn. But the students and others are required to spin during this year of purification by way of penance in order to popularise spinning and to add to the manufacture of hand-spun yarn so as to overtake full manufacture during the current year. The nation may be too lazy to do it. But if all put their hands to this work, it is incredibly easy, it involves very little sacrifice and saves an annual drain of sixty crores even if it does nothing else. I have discussed the matter with many mill-owners, several economists, men of business and no one has yet been able to challenge the position herein set forth. I do expect the 'Servant-of India' to treat a serious subject with seriousness and accuracy of information.

Y. I.—16th Feb. 1921.

A PLEA FOR SPINNING

A determined opposition was put up against the conditions regarding Swadeshi that were laid down in the civil disobedience resolution passed by the All-India Congress Committee at Delhi. It was directed against two requirements, namely, that the civil resister offering resistance in terms of that resolution was bound to know hand-spinning and use only hand-spun and hand-woven *khadi*; and that in the event of a district or tahsil offering civil disobedience *en masse* the district or the tahsil concerned must manufacture its own yarn and cloth by the hand. The opposition betrayed woeful ignorance of the importance of hand-spinning. Nothing but hand-spinning can banish pauperism from the land. Paupers cannot become willing sufferers. They have never known the pain of plenty to appreciate the happiness of voluntarily suffering hunger or other bodily discomfort. Swaraj for them can only mean ability to support themselves without begging. To awaken among them a feeling of discontent with their lot without providing them with the means of removing the cause thereof is to court certain destruction, anarchy, outrage and plunder in which they themselves will be the chief victims. Hand-spinning alone can possibly supply them with supplementary and additional earnings. Hand-weaving for many and carding for a limited number can provide complete livelihood. But hand-weaving is not a lost art. Several million men know hand-weaving. But very few know hand-spinning in the true sense of the term. Tens of thousands are, it is true, turning the wheel to-day but only a few are spinning yarn. The cry all over is that hand-spun yarn is not good enough for warp. Just as half-baked bread is no bread, even so ill-spun weak thread is no yarn. Thousands of men must know hand-spinning to be able in their respective districts to improve the quality of the yarn that is now being spun in the country. Therefore those who offer civil disobedience for the sake of establishing Swaraj must know hand-spinning. Mark, they are not required to turn out yarn every day. It would be well if they did. But they must know how to spin even properly twisted yarn. It was a happy omen to me, that in spite of the opposition the amendment was rejected by a large majority. One argument advanced in favour of rejection was, that the Sikh men considered it an undignified occupation to spin and looked down upon hand-weaving. I do hope that the sentiment is not representative of the brave community. Any community that despises occupations that bring an honest livelihood is a community going down an incline. If spinning has been the speciality of women, it is because they have more leisure and not because it is an inferior occupation. The underlying suggestion that a wielder of the sword will not wield the wheel is to take a distorted view of a soldier's calling. A man who lives by the sword does *not* serve his community even as the soldiers in the employ of the

Government do not serve the country. The wielding of the sword is an unnatural occupation resorted to among civilized people only on extraordinary occasions and only for self-defence. To live by hand-spinning and hand-weaving is any day more *manly* than to live by killing. Aurangzeb was not the less a soldier for sewing caps. What we prize in the Sikhs is not their ability to kill. The late Sardar Lachman Singh will go down to posterity as a hero, because he knew how to die. The Mahant of Nankhana Saheb will go down to posterity as a murderer. I hope therefore that no man will decline to learn the beautiful life-giving art of hand-spinning on the ground of its supposed inferiority.

Y. I.—10th Nov. 1921.

THE DUTY OF SPINNING

In " The Secret of Swaraj" I have endeavoured to show what home spinning means for our country. In any curriculum of the future, spinning must be a compulsory subject. Just as we cannot live without breathing and without eating, so is it impossible for us to attain economic independence and banish pauperism from this ancient land without reviving home-spinning. I hold the spinning wheel to be as much a necessity in every household as the hearth. No other scheme that can be devised will ever solve the problem of the deepening poverty of the people.

How then can spinning be introduced in every home? I have already suggested the introduction of spinning and systematic production of yarn in every national school. Once our boys and girls have learnt the art they can easily carry it to their homes.

But this requires organisation. A spinning wheel must be worked for twelve hours per day. A practised spinner can spin two tolas and a half per hour. The price that is being paid at present is on an average four annas per forty tolas or one pound of yarn *i.e.*, one pice per hour. Each wheel therefore should give three annas per day. A strong one costs seven rupees. Working, therefore, at the rate of twelve hours per day it can pay for itself in less than 38 days. I have given enough figures to work upon. Any one working at them will find the results to be startling.

If every school introduced spinning, it would revolutionize our ideas of financing education. We can work a school for six hours per day and give free education to the pupils. Supposing a boy works at the wheel for four hours daily, he will produce every day 10 tolas of yarn and thus earn for his school one anna per day. Suppose further that he maufactures very little during the first month, and that the school works only twenty six days in the month. He can earn after the first month Rs. 1-10 per month. A class of thirty boys would yield, after the first month, an income of Rs. 48-12 per month.

I have said nothing about literary training. It can be given during the two hours out of the six. It is easy to see that every school can be made self supporting without much effort and the nation can engage experienced teachers for its schools.

The chief difficulty in working out the scheme is the spinning wheel. We require thousands of wheels if the art becomes popular. Fortunately, every village carpenter can easily construct the machine. It is a serious mistake to order them from the Ashram or any other place. The beauty of spinning is that it is incredibly simple, easily learnt, and can be cheaply introduced in every village.

The course suggested by me is intended only for this year of purification and probation. When normal times are reached and Swaraj is established one hour only may be given to spinning and the rest to literary training. *Y. I.—2nd Feb. 1921.*

THE DUTY OF SPINNING

[SPEAKING at a monster meeting of students held in Mirzapur Park, Calcutta, Mahatma Gandhi appealed to them to withdraw from educational institutions. In the course of that speech he spoke on the duty of spinning, which portion is printed here.]

Our education has been the most deficient in two things. Those who framed our education code neglected the training of the body and the soul. You are receiving the education of the soul but the very fact of non-co-operation for non-co-operation is nothing less and nothing more than withdrawing from participation in the evil that this Government is doing and continuing to do. And if we are withdrawing from evil conscientiously, deliberately, it means that we are walking with our face towards God. That completes or begins the soul training. But seeing that our bodily education has been neglected, and seeing that India has become enslaved because India forgot the spinning wheel, and because India sold herself for a mess of pottage, I am not afraid to place before you, the young men of Bengal, the spinning wheel for adoption. And let a training in spinning and production of as much yarn as you can ever do constitute your main purpose and your main training during this year of probation. Let your ordinary education commence after Swaraj is established, but let every young man, and every girl, of Bengal consider it to be their sacred duty to devote all their time and energy to spinning. I have drawn attention to the parallel, that presents itself before us, from the war. *Y. I.—2nd Feb. 1921.*

THE DOCTRINE OF CHARKA

[THE opening session of the National College, Calcutta, under the auspices of the Board of Education, formed by Srijuts Chittaranjan Das, Jitendralal Banerjee and other non-co-operation leaders, took place on Friday the 4th February 1921. In opening this College, Mahatma Gandhi addressed the students and professors, from which the following is culled.]

We have sufficiently talked about Charka and how it is going to free India—how a nation that came through the Charka to this country as traders, merchants and travellers settled themselves down as rulers with our co-operation, and how non-co-operation and by means of that very Indian *Charka* they will go back to their own country if they cannot live as fellow-citizens in India.

There are peoples who say—" how can

you expect the Mahomedans to be non-violent." How, I do not want to speak out. I want the *Charka* itself to speak out. The whole Europe will know when we place these Charkas in our mosques. Something like 800 Charkas had been ordered for the mosques so that the people who come there should be able to produce Indian yarn with which Indian clothes should be woven by Indian hands in Indian homes to clothe our nakedness or at least to provide home-spun shrouds for us. Thus every revolution of the *Charka* I can assure you, will bring the success of this bloodless revolution the nearer every day. That is the doctrine of *Charka*. Therefore I ask you to work up this doctrine which will be a great advertisement both of our determination to win freedom, and if possible, through peaceful means.

If you are determined to have the freedom of your country, if you want to see the cessation of our slavery in which we are living for close upon two centuries, it requires from you a peaceful battle—the battle of the *Charka*. *Y. I.—9th Feb. 1921.*

THE MESSAGE OF THE CHARKA

THE *Indian Social Reformer* has published a note from a correspondent in praise of the spinning-wheel. The correspondent in the course of his remarks hopes, that the movement will be so organised that the spinners may not weary of it. Mr, Amritlal Thakkar in his valuable note (published in the *Servant of India*) on the experiment which he is conducting in Kathiawad, says that the charkha has been taken up by the peasant women. They are not likely to weary, for to them it is a source of livelihood to which they were used before. It had dried up, because there was no demand for their yarn. Townspeople who have taken to spinning may weary, if they have done so as a craze or a fashion. Those only will be faithful, who consider it their duty to devote their spare hours to doing what is to-day the most useful work for the country. The third class of spinners are the school-going children. I expect the greatest results from the experiment of introducing the charkha in the National Schools. If it is conducted on scientific lines by teachers who believe in the charkha as the most efficient means of making education available to the seven and a half lacs of villages in India, there is not only no danger of weariness, but every prospect of the nation being able to solve the problem of financing mass education without any extra taxation and without having to fall back upon immoral sources of revenue.

The writer in the *Indian Social Reformer* suggests, that an attempt should be made to produce finer counts on the spinning-wheel. I may assure him that the process has already begun, but it will be some time before we arrive at the finish of the Dacca muslin or even twenty counts. Seeing that hand-spinning was only revived last September, and India began to believe in it somewhat only in December, the progress it has made may be regarded as phenomenal.

The writer's complaint that hand-spun yarn is not being woven as fast as it is spun, is partly true. But the remedy is not so much to increase the number of looms, as to persuade the existing weavers to use hand-spun yarn. Weaving is a much more complex process than spinning. It is not, like spinning, only a supplementary industry, but a complete means of livelihood. It therefore never died out. There are *enough weavers and enough looms in India to replace the whole of the foreign import of cloth.* It should be understood that our looms—thousands of them in Madras, Maharashtra and Bengal —are engaged in weaving the fine yarn imported from Japan and Manchester. We *must* utilize these for weaving hand-spun yarn. And for that purpose, the nation has to revise its taste for the thin tawdry and useless muslins. I see no art in weaving muslins, that do not cover but only expose the body. Our ideas of art must undergo a change. But even if the universal weaving of thin fabric be considered desirable in normal conditions, at the present moment whilst we are making a mighty effort to become free and self-supporting, we must be content to wear the cloth that our hand-spun yarn may yield. We have therefore to ask the fashionable on the one hand to be satisfied with coarser garments; we must educate the spinners on the other hand to spin finer and more even yarn.

The writer pleads for a reduction in the prices charged by mill-owners for their manufactures. When lovers of Swadeshi begin to consider it their duty to wear khaddar, when the required number of spinning-wheels are working and the weavers are weaving hand-spun yarn, the mill-owners will be bound to reduce prices. It seems almost hopeless merely to appeal to the patriotism of those whose chief aim is to increase their own profits.

Incongruities pointed out by the writer such as the wearing of khaddar on public occasions and at other times of the most fashionable English suits, and the smoking of most expensive cigars by wearers of khaddar, must disappear in course of time, as the new fashion gains strength. It is my claim that as soon as we have completed the boycott of foreign cloth, we shall have evolved so far that we shall necessarily give up the present absurdities and remodel national life in keeping with the ideal of simplicity and domesticity implanted in the bosom of the masses. We will not then be dragged into an imperialism, which is built upon exploitation of the weaker races of the earth, and the acceptance of a giddy materialistic civilization protected by naval and air forces that have made peaceful living almost impossible. On the contrary, we shall then refine that imperialism, into a common wealth of nations which will combine, if they do, for the purpose of giving their best to the world and of protecting, not by brute force but by self-suffering, the weaker nations or races of the earth. Non-co-operation aims at nothing less than this revolution in the thought-world. Such a transformation can come only after the complete success of the spinning-wheel. India can become fit for delivering such a message, when she has become proof against temptation and therefore attacks from outside, by becoming self-contained regarding two of her chief needs—food and clothing.

Y. I.—29th June 1921.

THE CHARKA IN THE GITA

IN the last issue I have endeavoured to answer the objections raised by the Poet against spinning as a sacrament to be performed by all. I have done so in all humility and with the desire to convince the Poet and those who think like him. The reader will be interested in knowing, that my belief is derived largely from the Bhagavadgita. I have quoted the relevant verses in the article itself. I give below Edwin Arnold's rendering of the verses from his Song Celestial for the benefit of those who do not read Sanskrit.

Work is more excellent than idleness;
The body's life proceeds not, lacking work.
There is a task of holiness to do,
Unlike world-binding toil, which bindeth not
The faithful soul; such earthly duty do

Free from desire, and thou shalt well perform
Thy heavenly purpose. Spake Prajapati
In the beginning, when all men were made,
And, with mankind, the sacrifice—"Do this!
Work! Sacrifice! Increase and multiply
With sacrifice! This shall be Kamadhuk,
Your 'Cow of Plenty', giving back her milk
Of all abundance. Worship the gods thereby;
The gods shall yield ye grace. Those meats ye crave
The gods will grant to Labour, when it pays
Tithes in the altar-flame. But if one eats
Fruits of the earth, rendering to kindly heaven,
No gift of toil, that thief steals from his world."
Who eat of food after their sacrifice
Are quit of fault, but they that spread a feast

All for themselves, eat sin and drink
of sin.
By food the living live; food comes
of rain.
And rain comes by the pious sacrifice,
And sacrifice is paid with tithes of toil;
Thus action is of Brahma, who is one,
The Only, All—pervading; at all times
Present in sacrifice. He that abstains
To help the rolling wheels of this great
world,
Glutting his idle sense, lives a lost life,
Shameful and vain.

Work here undoubtedly refers to physical labour, and work by way of sacrifice can only be work to be done by all for the common benefit. Such work—such sacrifice can only be spinning. I do not wish to suggest, that the author of the Divine Song had the spinning wheel in mind. He merely laid down a fundamental principle of conduct. And reading in and applying it to India I can only think of spinning as the fittest and most acceptable sacrificial body labour. I cannot imagine anything nobler or more national than that for say one hour in the day we should all do the labour that the poor must do, and thus identify ourselves with them and through them with all mankind. I cannot imagine better worship of God than that in His name I should labour for the poor even as they do. The spinning wheel spells a more equitable distribution of the riches of the earth.

Y. I.—20th Oct. 1921.

SPINNING AS FAMINE RELIEF

Mrs. Jaiji Petit has sent the following notes of an experiment being conducted in spinning among the famine-stricken people at Miri near Ahmednagar. I gladly publish the notes as the experiment is being conducted under the supervision of an Englishwoman. The reader will not fail to observe the methodical manner in which the work is being done. All the difficulties have been met and provided for. Even the very small experiment shows what a potent instrument, the spinning wheel is for famine relief. Properly organised it cannot but yield startling results.— M. K. G.

In the month of August 1920, when the severity of the famine was being felt, the idea of introducing spinning as a famine relief to respectable middle class people was started and Miss Latham kindly gave a spinning wheel to introduce the work. Attempts were made to introduce the work especially among the Dhangars who were used to spinning wool but they proved futile. Spinning a thin thread of cotton was thought an impossibility in a village which did not know anything about it. Doubts were also entertained as to whether the work if taken up would be paying or at least helpful. In such different difficulties and objections, the wheel remained idle for nearly three months, and in spite of vigorous efforts no body seemed willing to take up the work. In December 1920, Miss Latham again sent four more wheels through the kindness of Mrs. J. Petit and some cotton. They were given for trial to different persons. Signs now seemed a little hopeful and at last one Ramoshi woman was prevailed upon to take up the work seriously. This was about the 20th of January 1921, since when the work has assumed a different shape. The example of this woman was copied by two more who undertook to take the work. Through great perseverance 4 lbs. of yarn were prepared by these three spinners and it was sent for sale. In the meantime many women began to make the inquiries and expressed a desire to take it up if it helped them financially in some way. A rate of spinning 6 as. a lb. was therefore fixed and it helped other spinners to join the work.

Here another difficulty viz. that of funds came in the way. All the five wheels were engaged and five more prepared locally were also engaged. The stock of cotton was also exhausted. It seemed that the work would suffer for want of funds to prepare wheels, purchase cotton, and pay the workers. Rao Bahadur Chitale personally saw this difficulty and helped the work with a grant of Rs. 100. Miss Latham, when she knew of this difficulty, kindly sent another hundred. These two grants came at the right time and gave a stimulus to the work. Local gentlemen helped with their own cotton.

The demand for wheels went on increasing day by day. People being too poor to pay for the wheels, it became necessary to get the wheels prepared locally and lend them to the workers. Twenty seven more wheels were prepared which also gave work to local carpenters who had no work on account of famine. One carpenter improved the wheel by making it more light and useful for finer yarn. The prices of the wheel were paid at Rs. 3, Rs. 3-8, and Rs. 4 per wheel according to the quality. Three of these wheels have been sold for Rs. 9-8. The total sum spent on these wheels is Rs. 103-8-0 which includes the sum for the wheels kindly sent by Mrs. Petit.

Though local cotton was secured for the work, it proved too bad for beginners. A new method therefore was introduced to improve the local cotton, which not only helped the work but also provided work for a few more persons. Raw cotton was secured and the dirt and the dry leaves in it were carefully removed before it was ginned. The rate for this work was fixed at one pice per lb. Any old man who did this work got an opportunity of earning one anna a day, by cleaning 4 lbs. of raw cotton. After it was thus cleaned, it was ginned with a hand-gin which gave work to some women who ginned, at the rate of one anna per 10 lbs. One woman could thus earn 2 as. and 6 pies each day. This ginned cotton was then cleaned by a *pinjari* who charged at the rate of one anna per pound and earned about 8 as. per day. It would have been better and easier too, if cotton had been purchased from the mills, but as this cleaning process of the local cotton provided work for a few workers, it was thought the more desirable in these days. A major portion of these cleaning charges is however made up by the sale of cotton seed secured after ginning. The following statement will show the expenses incurred for this and the price of raw cotton for every 60 lbs.

	RS. A. P.
Price of 60 lbs. of raw cotton @ 20 Rs. a patia (240 lbs.). ...	5—0—0
Removal of dirt, waste and dry leaves @ 1 pice per pound ...	0–15—0
Ginning of 52 lbs. of raw clean cotton @ 1 an. per 10 lbs. ...	0—5—3

	RS. A. P.
Cleaning the Lint (17 lbs.) by a pinjari @ 1 Anna per lb. ...	1—1—0
Total	7—4—3
Deduct price of cotton seed 35 lbs. @ 20 lbs. per Re.	1-12—0
Net charges for 17 lbs. of clean cotton	5—9—3

Thus the cost of one pound of cotton comes to 5 as. and 3 pies only. The proportion of waste viz. 8 lbs. in 60 lbs. of raw cotton is too high and could be avoided by securing better and cleaner cotton.

There are at present 29 wheels going and there is still a great demand for wheels. But the funds being limited, more wheels could not be prepared and provided. Spinning is done by those who absolutely know nothing about it previously. Consequently the yarn is still of an inferior sort. It is improving day by day but if a competent teacher could be secured, it would improve rapidly. Amongst the spinners, some are full-time workers and others are leisure-time workers.

About two lbs. of yarn are now prepared every day and the quantity will increase as the spinners get used to the work. The rate for spinning is fixed at 6 as. a lb., though many workers complain that it is not enough. As the yarn sent for sale realised a price of As. 12 a pound, the spinning charges could not be increased without a loss. Every lb. of yarn requires Annas 11 pies 3 for expenses, as 0-5-3 for cotton and 0-6-0 for spinning. Thus every lb. leaves a profit of 9 pies only. The establishment and other charges are not calculated. With the present rate of spinning at 6 as. a lb., one spinner earns 3 as. per day by spinning 20 to 24 tolas, more earn 2 as. a day by spinning 15 tolas and the rest 1½ as. a day for 10 tolas, the beginners excluded. The more the spinner is used to the work, the more he will earn.

An attempt was made to prepare cloth out of the yarn and three and a half lbs. of yarn were given to a weaver for weaving. He however charged an exorbitant rate for weaving. He prepared nine and a half yards of cloth and charged Rs. 3-9 for it practically 1 rupee a lb. The cloth cost Rs. 6-0-6 and was sold at Rs. 6-3-0, with a profit of as. 2 and pies 6 only. To obviate the difficulty about weaving, a separate room with one teacher to teach weaving to local persons is urgently required. Many local people wish to learn this art. A separate loom will reduce the cost of the cloth prepared on it below the prevailing market rate. About 6 lbs. of yarn are given to different weavers to ascertain the exact charges, but all this difficulty can only be removed by having a special loom.

When there was a shortage of cotton and the workers had no work, wool was introduced for spinning till cotton was ready. This work was willingly taken up by the Dhangar. They were however required to spin finer thread of wool than they usually prepared. They took some time to pick up the work, and now there are 10 wool spinners working fine thread. They are also paid at 6 as. a lb. for spinning. Wool worth Rs. 31 @ 2 lbs. a rupee was purchased, and though the cotton was ready, the wool spinning was continued by starting a separate department, as the Dhangars readily took up the work. The whole process of cleaning the wool is also done by the Dhangar women, who get an extra anna per lb. for it. The sorting of wool is carefully looked to. The majority of wool spinners use their own spinning wheels but a few are now asking for the improved wheel for preparing finer threads.

Dhangar weavers being locally available blankets after the Pandharpur and Dawangiri pattern are being prepared from this finer thread and different designs have been suggested to them. The Dhangars being a stubborn race do not readily adopt the new improvement. But this work has set them to work up new designs of blankets which will permanently help them in their own profession. They now require a broader and improved loom and instruction in colouring wool. Efforts are made to secure a clever full time weaver who will introduce a better method of weaving. Two blankets were prepared and sold at cost price, one for Rs. 5-13-6 and the other for Rs. 6-6-0. Orders are being received for blankets now, but to continue the work would require some funds.

To keep so many persons working is not only an ideal form of famine relief, but a means to promote village industries, and remove the demoralising effects of successive famines. Thus stands the work of about one month. It now requires an improved handloom, a good teacher, a special loom for wool, more spinning wheels (which the neighbouring villagers are also demanding) and many other things. The work is going on vigorously and it is hoped will not be allowed to suffer for want of funds. *Y. I.—11th May 1921.*

THE POTENCY OF THE SPINNING-WHEEL

NO amount of human ingenuity can manage to distribute water over the whole land, as a shower of rain can. No irrigation department, no rules of precedence, no inspection and no water-cess. Every thing is done with an ease and a gentleness that by their very perfection evade notice. The spinning-wheel, too, has got the same power of distributing work and wealth in millions of houses in the simplest way imaginable. Those of us who do not know what it is to earn a livelihood by the sweat of one's brow, may consider the three annas a day as a pittance beneath the consideration of any man. They do not know that even in these days of high prices, there are districts in India where even three annas a day would be a boon to the poor. But we must not consider the question of the spinning-wheel merely from the point of individual earnings. The spinning-wheel is a force in national regeneration. If we wish for real Swaraj, we must achieve economic independence. Boycott of foreign cloth is its negative aspect. For this we must produce cloth sufficient to clothe the country. This can only be done by hand-spinning. All the mills that we have got, will not be able together to cope with the situation. If all rush for the thin mill-made cloth, it will rise in price beyond the capacity of the poor, and the experience of 1907-08 will be repeated. Moreover, the cloth best suited for the three seasons of India is *Khadi.* Those who have used *Khadi* during this summer, have come to realise, that after the soft clean touch of *Khadi* it is impossible to use sticky Malmal or twills. *Khadi* can enable its wearer to withstand the cold of an average winter as even wool cannot. The climate of India demands that clothes be washed as often as possible. Only *Khadi* can stand this constant wash. *Khadi* was once the dress of the nation at large. One must see to believe how venerable the old Patels and Deshmukhs looked when dressed in home-spun *Khadi.* There are instances of whole villages taking a legitimate pride in the fact that they had to import nothing but salt in the whole round of the six seasons. With such conditions, there could be no drain, no exploitation and therefore no Para-raj. A little village could make terms with the rulers of the land consistent with its self-respect, dignity and independence. Is our love of luxury so inveterate, that we cannot control it even for the sake of Swaraj? *Y. I.—6th July 1921.*

THE WHEEL OF FORTUNE

[A certain correspondent from Sindh writing to Mahatma Gandhi puts the question, "Will the spinning wheel solve the problem of India's poverty? If it will, how?" Here is his answer.]

I am more than ever convinced that without the spinning wheel the problem of India's poverty cannot be solved. Millions of India's peasants starve for want of supplementary occupation. If they have spinning to add to their slender resources, they can fight successfully against pauperism and famine. Mills cannot solve the problem. Only hand-spinning—and nothing else—can. When India was forced to give up hand-spinning, she had no other occupation in return. Imagine what would happen to a man who found himself suddenly deprived of a quarter of his bare livelihood. Over eighty-five percent of Her population have more than a quarter of their time lying idle. And, therefore, even apart from the terrible drain rightly pointed out by the Grand Old Man of India, she has steadily grown poorer because of this enforced idleness. The problem is how to utilise these billions of hours of the nation without disturbing the rest. Restoration of the spinning wheel is the only possible answer. This has nothing to do with my special views on machinery or with the boycott of foreign goods in general. India is likely to accept the answer in full during this year. It is madness to tinker with the problem. I am writing this in Puri in front of the murmuring waves. The picture of the crowd of men, women, and children, with their fleshless ribs under the very shadow of Jagannath, haunts me. If I had the power, I would suspend every other activity in schools, and colleges, and everywhere else, and popularise spinning; prepare out of these lads and lasses spinning teachers: inspire every carpenter to prepare spinning wheels; and ask the teachers to take these life-going machines to every home, and teach them spinning. If I had the power, I would stop an ounce of cotton from being exported and would have it turned into yarn in these homes. I would dot India with depots for receiving this yarn and distributing it among weavers. Given sufficient steady and trained workers, I would undertake to drive pauperism out of India during this year. This undoubtedly requires a change in the angle of vision and in the national taste. I regard the Reforms and everything else in the nature of opiates to deaden our conscience. We must refuse to wait for generations to furnish us with a patient solution of a problem which is ever-growing in seriousness. Nature knows no mercy in dealing stern justice. If we do not wake up before long, we shall be wiped out of existence. I invite the sceptics to visit Orissa, penetrate its villages, and find out for themselves where India stands. They will then believe with me that to possess, or to wear, an ounce of foreign cloth is a crime against India and humanity. I am able to restrain myself from committing suicide by starvation, only because I have faith in India's awakening, and her ability to put herself on the way to freedom from this desolating pauperism. Without faith in such a possibility, I should cease to take interest in living. I invite the questioner, and every other intelligent lover of his country, to take part in this privileged national service in making spinning universal by introducing it in every home, and make it profitable for the nation by helping to bring about a complete boycott of foreign cloth during this year. I have finished the questions and endeavoured to answer them. The most important from the practical stand-point was the one regarding spinning. I hope, I have demonstrated the necessity of home-spinning as the only means of dealing with India's poverty. I know, however, that innumerable difficulties face a worker in putting the doctrine into execution. The most difficult, perhaps, is that of getting a proper wheel. Save in the Punjab where the art is still alive, the difficulty is very real. The carpenters have forgotten the construction and the innocent workers are at their wit's end. The chief thing undoubtedly, therefore, is for the worker to make himself acquainted with the art and the handling of spinning wheels. I lay down some simple tests for testing them. No machine that fails to satisfy the tests should be accepted or distributed.

(1) The wheel must turn easily, freely, and noiselessly.

(2) The turning handle must be rigidly fixed to the axle.

(3) The post must be properly driven home and joints well-fixed.

(4) The spindle must turn noiselessly and without a throb in its holders. Jarring sound cannot be avoided unless the holders are made of knit straw as in the Punjab, or of tough leather.

(5) No machine is properly made unless it manufactures in the hands of a practised spinner at least 2½ tolas of even and properly twisted yarn of six counts in an hour. I know a youngster, who has not had more than per-

haps three months' practice, having been able to spin 2½ tolas of the above quality of yarn in 35 minutes. No machine should be given until it has been worked at least full one hour in the manner suggested and found satisfactory. *Y. I.—6th April 1921.*

THE SPINNING WHEEL

[On February 15, 1922, Mahatma Gandhi has addressed the following letter to Sir Daniel Hamilton from Bardoli on the Spinning Wheel.]

Dear Sir,

Mr. Hodge writes to me to say that you would like to have an hour's chat with me, and he has suggested that I should open the ground which I gladly do. I will not take up your time by trying to interest you in any other activity of mine except the spinning wheel. Of all my outward activities, I do believe that the spinning wheel is of the most permanent and the most beneficial. I have abundant proof now to support my statement that the spinning wheel will solve the problem of economic distress in millions of India's homes, and it constitutes an effective insurance, against famines.

You know the great Scientist Dr. P. C. Ray, but you may not know that he has also become an enthusiast on behalf of the spinning wheel. India does not need to be industrialized in the modern sense of the term. It has 7,50,000 villages scattered over a vast area 1,900 miles long, 1,500 miles broad. The people are rooted to the soil, and the vast majority are living a hand-to-mouth life. Whatever may be said to the contrary, having travelled throughout the length and breadth of the land with eyes open, and having mixed with millions, there can be no doubt that pauperism is growing. There is no doubt also that the millions are living in enforced idleness for at least 4 months in the year. Agriculture does not need revolutionary changes. The Indian peasant requires a supplementary industry. The most natural is the introduction of the spinning wheel, not the hand-loom. The latter cannot be introduced in every home, whereas the former can, and it used to be so even a century ago. It was driven out not by economic pressure but by force deliberately used as can be proved from authentic records. The restoration, therefore, of the spinning wheel solves the economic problem of India at a stroke. I know that you are a lover of India, that you are deeply interested in the economic and moral uplift of my country. I know too that you have great influence. I would like to enlist it on behalf of the spinning wheel. It is the most effective force for introducing successful Co-Operative Societies. Without honest co-operation of the millions, the enterprise can never be successful, and as it is already proving a means of weaning thousands of women from a life of shame, it is as moral an instrument as it is economic.

I hope you will not allow yourself to be prejudiced by anything you might have heard about my strange views about machinery. I have nothing to say against the development of any other industry in India by means of machinery but I do say that to supply India with cloth manufactured either outside or inside through gigantic mills is an economic blunder of the first magnitude just as it would be to supply cheap bread through huge bakeries established in the chief centres in India and to destroy the family stove.

Yours faithfully,
M. K. GANDHI.

APPENDICES

BY

MAGANLAL K. GANDHI

A MODEL WEAVING-SCHOOL

ALL the external activities of Satyagrahashram in connection with Swadeshi have for some time now been taken over by the Gujarat Provincial Congress Committee. People, who are in need of or wish to know anything about ginning-wheels, spinning-wheels, looms and Khadi, are requested to correspond with the Secretary of the Khadi department of that Committee. The Ashram now only conducts a weaving-school, which teaches all the processes from ginning right up to weaving. The boys of the Ashram school are at present taking the full course of instruction here, and we have not the room to take up students from outside. Some description of the work done is given here in the hope, that it may perhaps furnish suggestions to outside students and to schools desirous of having spinning-classes attached to them.

Forty-nine spinning wheels are here regularly at work, over and above twenty-five others which are reserved for beginners. All these are worked three to six hours per day. Some are worked for even seven or eight hours. After a month's training, a friend worked twelve to fourteen hours daily for a number of days and thus proved the possibility of earning three annas a day. Another, a sister, spun nine to ten hours daily for some days after finishing her round of domestic business. In a month and a half, she had spun enough to get *sadlas* and other cloth woven out of yarn spun by herself, and actually began wearing these things. She is now-a-days spinning at the rate of eight hours a day. One day there was something wrong with this lady's *rentia*. She referred the matter to the present writer who set it right. But she was not satisfied. She complained again, and again was the *rentia* operated upon. But the wheel apparently suffered from some occult malady, which she was at a loss to diagnose. Every time its spinning power would get enfeebled. At last the poor lady lost all patience and was almost ready to weep. This was reported to me, and this time I examined the wheel very critically and effected a perfect cure. It now moved merrily, and merrily did the sister proceed with her work. It is very desirable that all the wheels in a spinning-class be kept in a perfect condition. When that is the case, the spinner does not tire and works cheerfully and speedily. Our class is attended by five ladies, who spin five or six hours every day, and by twenty-three students of the Ashram school, of whom eighteen are boys and five are girls. The conduct of this class is not an easy job. Their spirits are in continual need of cheering. Some of them spin very rapidly. But sometimes there is a grievous attack of head-ache, at other times the still more grievous attack of idleness.

Sometimes the hand is fatigued, at other times the wheel gets out of repair.

We are now replacing the thick by a thin spindle. It is true that with the slightest interference or rough handling, this thin spindle bends and begins to wobble. But it makes the movement of the wheel very smooth and easy, and also adds to its speed, as the revolutions are doubled from the fifty of the thick spindle to a hundred in the thin spindle following from one revolution of the large wheel. The doubling of revolutions does not mean a double output, but there is certainly a considerable increase. With the thick spindle, the wheel must go through 8 or 10 revolutions for the drawing and winding of one length of yarn; with the thin spindle, the revolutions of the wheel needed for that purpose are reduced to 4 or 5. Hence with the thin spindle, there is an economy of labour. The speed of drawing the yarn by the hand is clearly limited, so that 200 or 300 revolutions of the spindle instead of 100 would not double or treble the speed or the output. Advanced students draw and wind two feet to two feet and a half of yarn every five seconds. This comes to 8 to 10 yards a minute. If the sliver is good and the student in a spinning-mood, there is less breakage of yarn. Even considering the time lost on account of breakage and joining, some students are easily able to spin 400 to 500 yards of yarn of about 12 counts, fit for warp. This approximates to the speed of a mill spindle, and is therefore quite satisfactory. When the work is over, the student removes the spindle from the wheel and keeps it in good preservation. Yet accidents do occur. The class master must know how to repair a spindle which has thus gone wrong. He must also know how to put the wheel in good working order. The string which makes the spindle revolve often breaks, but if it is well-twisted, treated with wax, and then rubbed well with a piece of cloth, it becomes more durable and lasts for a number of days.

The students generally like to work on the *rentia*. But the moment it gets a little wrong and cannot be soon corrected, they rise and flee. Not only the beginners but even advanced scholars are sometimes confused, when called upon to set right such a simple machine as the spinning-wheel. A veteran leader who set the non-co-operating students of engineering at work upon the spinning-wheel, made the remark that English education has incapacitated our young men. It was with great pain that he said this. And it is the simple truth of the matter. We can clearly see, that as a result of this education, we have not only lost the power of our hands and feet, but we also lack in patience and perseverance. We cannot bear to take the trouble of correcting anything that is wrong. Newspaper leader-writers question the educative value of spinning and doubt its efficacy in driving away poverty from our midst. Their doubts would vanish if ever they tried and saw for themselves what children gain from the spinning-wheel. But these writers are themselves the product of English education. To expect them to be patient, is to forget the character of the discipline to which they have been subject. There is no better test than the spinning-wheel, if we wish to ascertain whether our children are educated in the real and the proper sense of that term.

Many people still question the economic value of hand spinning. But I believe that the results of our experiments may perhaps lead them to reconsider their views. I will here put down the statistics of our own class. Among our students, there are five playful children, who spin only when the spirit possesses them. But all of them spin good yarn fit for warp. Hardly any spin yarn below 10 counts. Many spin yarn of about 15 counts. Now-a-days the boys are giving four hours to spinning. Formerly they used to work six hours daily, but then there was a tendency to occasional slackness. Now we have ruled that when once a student has spun a length of 1000 yards, he may be allowed to leave the spinning class, and learn carding etc. This arrangement has had excellent efforts. All spin without losing a moment and spin 1000 yards in two to four hours according to the skill acquired. And the yarn thus produced is pretty uniform, well twisted, and fit for warp. We have fixed a round wire frame on the axle of the wheel just near the handle, with a circumference of 4 feet. This frame is used for opening the cone into a hank. 750 revolutions of this mean a thousand yards of yarn. Most students count the revolutions, while they are moving the frame, and hence do not take much additional time for calculations. Some are not able to practice this, and they count the length after they have prepared the hank.

1000 yards of yarn of six counts weigh 8 *tolas.* (840 yards make a hank. If six such hanks weigh a pound, the yarn is of 6 counts. Hence 840 yards of six count of yarn weigh 6⅔ *tolas.*) 4 annas is a quite proper wage for spinning one pound of six-count yarn of a standard quality. This means a wage of nine pies and a half for spinning 8 *tolas.* But most of our students spin yarn of 12 to 15 counts, and even finer. And this is quite good and fit for weaving. The wage for a thousand yards of finer yarn must be proportionately higher; as the finer the yarn, the greater the number of twists to be given to it. Twelve-count yarn requires nearly half as much twisting again as six-count yarn. Hence the wage of a thousand yards of twelve-count yarn must be half as much again as that of the same length of six-count yarn. But this proportionately higher wage makes the hand-spun yarn much dearer than the mill-made yarn of the same count. If we take 8 and 12 annas to be the wage for spinning a pound of yarn of 12 and 16 counts respectively, the wage for spinning a length of 1000 yards of the same counts will be 10 or 11 pies. One student spins this amount in 2 hours, several in 3 hours and the rest in 4.

On the last *Amavasya* it was twenty two days since the students set regularly to work after the *vaishaka* vacation. Deducting three holidays on Sundays and three half-holidays on Wednesdays, we get seventeen and a half working days. There was an average attendance of twenty two students out of twenty three. Twenty two students spun in seventeen days and a half twenty four *shers* and a half of yarn of about fourteen counts. If we take ten annas to be the average wage for spinning a *sher*, this comes to fifteen rupees and four annas. This is exclusive of Rs. 1-11-0 which is the wage of 18 pounds of cotton carded and made into slivers by one student in 12 days, calculated at an anna and a half per pound. It is also exclusive of the extra work put in by students on five or six days after finishing their daily quota of 1000 yds. of yarn by way of carding and opening yarn for weaving tapes and carpets. These students gave some of their private time also to this work.

There is no doubt, that the figures will mount higher when the students acquire the habit of methodical work. But whatever the pecuniary value of their work might be, method in work itself will be an acpuisition beyond all price.

So much for the spinning department. I hope to be able to deal with the weaving department on another occasion.

Y. I.—21st July 1921.

SPINNING DEPARTMENT

I should like to add a few more facts about the spinning department, before I come to weaving.

In *Ashadha* the students were more energetic than before. The number of regular students was 21, and these in 23 working days (there being six holidays in the month) spun 30 pounds and 24 *tolas* of yarn of about 12 counts on the average, fit for warp. At ten annas a pound, this means a wage of Rs. 19-2-0. The total number of hours of spinning was 1337. At 4 hours a day it should have been 1932 (23 number of days × 21 number of students × 4). This deficiency is not due to idleness, nor to headache. Complaints of idleness have now quite ceased. And students now understand that headache may prevent one from reading or working sums but not from spinning. They have also realised that if the arms are fatigued by fetching water or swimming, there is nothing like spinning for removing the fatigue. The thing is that those students who have mastered spinning were engaged in carding and other process. If full time had been given to spinning, we would have turned out a proportionately bigger quantity of yarn.

The spinning power of the students is increasing every day. The students who spun 7 *tolas* an hour during the Satyagraha week ís now no longer a prodigy and others are fast overtaking him. One day a girl spun 9 *tolas* of uniform and well-twisted 12-count yarn in 6 hours. At the above rate this means a wage of 2 annas 3 pies. For 8 hours therefore the wage would be 3 annas, for 12 hours 4 annas 6pies, for 14 hours 5 annas 3 pies. But it is hardly necessary to emphasise the pecuniary value of the work, so far as schools are concerned. The point is that by constituting spinning as a permanent part of our school curricula we provide manual training of the highest kind and at the same time prepare for the re-advent of a day when spinning will be as much a part of our domestic economy as say cooking.

Y. I.—11th Aug. '21.

THE ADVANTAGE OF THE THIN SPINDLE

Since we introduced the thin Spindle, we have been keeping a number of them in reserve. When a student has his spindle bent, it is not corrected there and then but he is at once given one of the spare good ones, so there is no delay. Afterwards all the spindles that have gone wrong are collected and corrected together.

The *sadi*, i.e. the wrapping on the spindle which serves as a pulley, is often cut by itself and has sometimes to be cut off in order to correct the spindle. A new *sadi* has to be wrapped and for this a bottle of thick gum is kept ready at hand. It must be made of fine strong yarn, and be wrapped very tight. If it is loose, the string which revolves the spindle (*mala*) sinks in it and cuts it as under, and at once the spindle stops. If the *sadi* is made of coarse yarn, it becomes rough, and so the *mala* does not run smoothly, and the spindle throbs and causes breakage of the yarn while it is being spun.

Pairs of *chamarakhan* (leather-bearing) also are kept in reserve. When these become too soft by an excess of oiling or by rough handling, they must be changed. Now-a-days we make them from raw hides and not from leather or bamboo, and so they keep longer.

Formerly a round piece of wood or card-board used to serve as a rest for winding the cone. But now we have substituted a piece of horn which is more durable. Wax is kept in stock for treating the *mala*. Besides these things we have a small oil-can, a pen-knife, a hammer, a chisel, and a small anvil.

The students bring the hank twisted hard in the shape of a stick. The hank weighs two *tolas*, which is the standard weight of the sliver provided. A bigger hank causes trouble while we open it, and the yarn is spoilt. The yarn spun by each student is kept separate with his name upon a wooden tag attached to it. Every student is asked to stick to one particular count all along till he has spun out enough for a length of warp; and then the yarn is sent to the weaving department. Every one is anxious to see when his yarn is sent out for weaving. Three such lengths of warp are being woven at present. About seven are ready waiting to be woven. An eleven year old girl will soon get a piece 20 yards long and 42 inches wide out of yarn spun by herself in the course of three months. This will provide her with too suits of clothing of two small *sadis*, 2 blouses and 2 petticoats. Her father had put in a pound of yarn spun by himself, to finish up the piece, and in return for this, she is going to spare a *dhoti* for him too. She is as much pleased to see the cloth woven from her own yarn as most girl would be to see brocade. Two other girls have combined their stock of yarn and are daily asking for it to be woven. Those students who have passed out from the spinning class are engaged in other departments, and have not much time to spare for spinning; so they work on holidays and prepare woof for their own warps, which are waiting to be woven. So in the second month, the spinning department is in full swing. Y. *I.—18th Aug. 1921.*

HAND-LOOMS

The working of the spinning class having been fully described in the first two articles, the process next to be taken up is carding; but having received a number of queries as to the working of hand-looms, I propose to deal with this before going into intermediate processes.

Questions are asked as to which will be the most useful loom for weaving hand-spun yarn. Some want our opinion about the automatic looms; others insist upon the necessity of inventing a new swift-working machine, while still others ask for monetary help to prepare such after their own designs.

My humble but firm opinion is that the old pit-loom is the best, especially for weaving hand-spun yarn. No doubt it is the slowest working instrument but is the surest of all, and just as our old spinning-wheel in spite of its being the slowest instrument is absolutely capable of spinning out all the cotton that India produces to-day, so the old pit-loom is perfectly capable of weaving out all the yarn that India can produce by means of the spinning wheels and the mills.

This is not the time to enter into the figures in support of my statement. I shall only try to show the usefulness of the pit-loom. The fly-shuttle loom has its place in the sphere of home industry as well as of the factory, but the automatic looms have no room in this industry. Its drawbacks can only be realized by a study of the facts and figures regarding concerns which employ such looms. People who newly take up this industry should beware of flashy advertisements. They should not be misled by professed calculations of the working of such looms.

The fly-shuttle looms have varying adjustments. In the Muzzaffarpur spinning and weaving exhibition held in May last, a party from this school was present with its wheel and loom. Of all the fly-shuttle looms exhibited, the one from this school was selected as the simplest and lightest of all. It is all made of wood, with the exception of nails and screws required for joining. The pickers are also made entirely of wood. The shuttle and perns are home-made. Other looms had iron bars in their boxes, were operated with foreign shuttles, and their perns were unwieldy. Our loom is modelled upon a type of looms working in thousands in the Madras Presidency. The whole loom with a wooden frame to fit on a pit, with the exception of the hields and reed costs Rs. 45 These latter things are not supplied, as there is no fixed standard of the yarn to be used on it.

I wish some public spirited person or firm will come forward in Madras or elsewhere in that presidency and undertake to supply the fly-shuttle loom as described above promptly and at reasonable rates. Any one desirous of taking up this work may correspond with the head of the *Khadi* Department, Gujarat Provincial Congress Commitee Ahmedabad.

Thus far as regards the fly-shuttle looms. I suggest to new manufacturers that they cannot do better than start with the old fashioned pit-looms. It is our experience that on account of less breakage of yarn, especially hand-spun yarn, the output of a pit-loom almost equals and in some cases even exceeds that of the fly-shuttle loom. In weaving broader width, however, the fly-shuttle is certainly more convenient. And when the hand-spun yarn is of good test, it enjoys a decided advantage over the old loom in point of swiftness. But we have to remember that we have got to deal with hand-spun yarn which is not likely to have a good test for some time to come. It is therefore that the old loom is the safest and surest weaving instrument to go on with for the present.

Y. I.—25th Aug. 1921.

WHAT KIND OF LOOM?

Questions are asked as to the production of cloths in an old-fashioned loom from handspun yarn. The experience in our school is, that a well-practised worker weaves on a pit-loom one yard cloth of 30 inches width and of fairly thick texture in one hour. Cloth of greater or smaller width varies in proportion. Our fly-shuttle pit-loom has not exceeded this figure in handspun yarn so far. When formerly we used mill-made yarn, it yielded about half as much cloth again as the old pit-loom. However in weaving *dhotiyans* and *sadis* from handspun as well as mill-made yarn the flyshuttle is very handy.

Then there is a question as to the necessity of beaming the yarn. We believe, that where there is no question of room, beaming should be dispensed with. Handloom weaving factories situated in thickly populated towns where rates of house-rent are very high, have reason to resort to beaming; but where space allows stretching of the yarn as practised by the professional weavers, it is a time-saving method and is artistic as well. There is an argument in favour of beaming that it allows of the handling of warp as long as 200 or even 300 yards. But if such length of handspun yarn can be prepared, it is equally easy, if not easier, to stretch it in the old style.

SIZING HANDSPUN YARN

It is said, that the difficulty of sizing handspun yarn is a serious handicap from which the movement suffers. As a matter of fact, the method of sizing it should be no different from that of sizing mill-made yarn. It is slipshod spinning which is at the bottom of this difficulty. The best way out of it is to organise and improve the production of handspun yarn. It is superstition to say that the yarn spun on the *charkha* cannot be strong and even. Where proper care is taken, it does improve and even surpass mill-made yarn in some respects. Punjab and Marwaḍ, where spinning has been carried on from past times, have also to improve their yarn. Not that the spinners there do not know their work, but they as well as the merchants who purchase their yarn are careless about the quality of the yarn turned out. Unless this work is taken up by men imbued with the true Swadeshi spirit, the condition is not likely to improve. The spinners should be visited at their work from time to time, and proper instructions as to the required twist and test to be given to the yarn should be imparted to them. The payment of a reasonably higher wage than the present is another way of improving the yarn. The wages we have arranged for our guidance are given below in the form of a table. Where living is cheaper than in Gujarat, they can be adjusted accordingly. The yarn having improved, the difficulty of sizing will disappear.

When a country weaver shows inability to weave hand-spun yarn, it means that he cannot weave it in the same reed space as he uses for the mill-made yarn. This is quite evident. The hand-spun yarn not being even, it requires wider reed space. The table given below also shows the number of ends of different counts to be drawn in an inch of a reed. Then if the cloth to be woven is meant for shirting or coating and not for *dhotiyan* or *sadi*, and if the yarn has a good test, two to four ends can be added to the number denoted in the table.

Count.	Test.	Wage per pound.	Approximate twist per inch.	Rounds on 4 feet hank frame.	Number of ends in an inch of reed.	Number of double ends in an inch.	Rates of weaving per square yard. Rs.	A.	P.
6	Warp	0 4 0	10	96	24 to 28	18 to 22	0	4	0
6	Weft	0 3 0	8	,,	...	...		...	
9	Warp	0 6 0	12	144	26 to 32	20 to 24	0	4	6
9	Weft	0 4 6	10	,,	...	...		...	
12	Warp	0 10 0	14	192	30 to 34	22 to 26	0	5	0
12	Weft	0 8 0	12	,,	...	...		...	
16	Warp	0 12 0	16	256	34 to 38	24 to 28	0	5	6
16	Weft	0 10 0	13	,,	...	...		...	
20	Warp	1 0 0	18	320	40 to 44	28 to 32	0	6	0
20	Weft	0 13 0	15	,,	...	...		...	

If the yarn is very weak and uneven, it should be woven with two ends in warp as well as in weft. This will give a strong texture to the cloth, making the process of weaving easy at the same time. The proportion in this case of ends to be drawn in an inch of the reed space is also given in the above table. If this course is adopted, heaps of handspun yarn that have accumulated all over the country can be woven out without much difficulty.

As a fact, the method of sizing traditionally followed by the weavers cannot be improved upon. Their selection of the sizing material is appropriate to the climate, season and circumstances. For the most part they use the staple corn. Jawari and maize being the cheapest are used in many parts. In the rainy season, however, they use wheat flour as a stronger sizing material to counteract the over-softening influence of the moisture present in the air. In the Madras Presidency, a cereal called *ragi* with a yellowish flour is used for coarse counts, while rice is used for finer counts. Rice and wheat are the best ingredients for sizing. The proportion used is from 10 per cent required for fine yarn to 20 per cent for coarse yarn.

Different preparations of various sizing materials are as follow:—

Wheat: Weigh the warp first. Then according to its fineness or coarseness, take fine wheat flour or *Menda* from 10 to 20 per cent of its weight, knead it well with water to form a thin paste, taking care that no lump remains. Boil some water just enough to soak the warp, then add the paste previously prepared and keep on stirring till the granules are well-cooked and the whole substance is reduced to the form of thin gruel. To every such preparation of one pound of flour, one ounce of sesamum or sweet oil should be added. This will give softness and smoothness to the threads of the warp and keep them from sticking to one another. Cocoanut or castor oil is also used as a lubricant. Any of these is good, except only that the castor oil will give a bad odour and a dull colour to the warp. The size thus prepared is then slowly poured on to the warp, which is kept folded on a gunny cloth or a clean slab. The warp is beaten with both the hands, while the process of pouring is going on, and when it is thoroughly saturated all over, it is spread out in the open and brushed repeatedly in one direction, often bringing the down side up till it gets dried. One or two or more persons according to the length of the warp are engaged in brushing, while several others are joining broken threads and shifting the sticks in the warp from one lease to another.

This is the most thorough of all the methods of sizing. The ends of fibres lying loose on every thread of the warp are straightened, and stuck fast round the thread by the process of brushing. The thread is rendered smooth and strong like wire, and the work of weaving is made all the easier by it. Thus swiftness in weaving is ensured. To master this requires long practice but it is worth the while of every student to do so. For an energetic youth about three hours' work under an expert every morning for two months or so is sufficient. With two assistants or more he will then be able to manage the brush-sizing himself without the aid of an expert. A less active person will take four or six months' practice.

The preparation of size from jawari and maize flour is just the same as from wheat flour, except that the flour of these cereals not being so fine as wheat flour, a larger quantity is required in their case.

Some people advise that wheat flour should be soaked for at least two days before it is boiled with water. It is said that the adherent quality of the flour is enhanced by this process.

Rice. The preparation from rice is simpler still. The required quantity of rice is boiled well with a quantity of water larger than that used for ordinary cooking and is allowed to remain for 12 to 24 hours. It is then strained through a piece of cloth tied over or into the mouth of a large vessel, more water being added as required in the process of straining. The strained matter is then reduced to consistent thinness; then oil is added to it in proportion as described above.

Rice is sometimes preferred to wheat, as it gives besides strength a fine gloss to the warp.

The thing to be borne in mind is that the yarn meant for preparing warp must be made thoroughly absorbent beforehand. For this, all the hanks must be connected in the form of one chain. It is then folded together, placed into a big vessel, whether of earth or metal, containing water enough to soak the yarn and then well pressed with both the feet for some time. It is left in this condition for two or three days, during which period it is beaten with a wooden club on a slab twice every day. It should be remembered that, unless it is beaten, it does not soak through for days. If it is not soaked well, it is incapable of absorbing the sizing material, and is imperfectly sized. The cotton fibre has a natural oily coating on it, which is removed by soaking it as described before or by boiling it for some time. It does not become thoroughly absorbent, till it is treated in this manner. After two or three days, when the yarn is well soaked, the chain is opened out and dried in shade, every hank being hung separately on a bamboo. Before it gets completely dried, it is well shaken with both the hands twice or thrice, so that the threads do not stick to one another. The Madrasi weavers are used to pouring rice water (generally thrown away when the rice is boiled) on the yarn, before it is dried out in the manner described above. This gives greater strength to the yarn, and causes less breakage in the process of winding and preparing it into warp.

The other method of sizing resorted to by the weavers is called hank-sizing. It is an easy process, and though not so efficient as brush-sizing, it answers well if carefully performed. In this case the yarn, before it is made up into a warp, is soaked, hank by hank, into the size prepared from wheat or rice as described above, and after pressing off the size a little from the hank with the thumb and a finger, the hank, wet as it is, is wound up on a bobbin. The warp is prepared immediately, while the bobbin is wet, each thread drying on the warping sticks as soon as another is drawn out. The warp thus prepared is fit for weaving.

We have tried hank-sizing in a weak solution of ordinary gum. It works well in dry season, but makes the yarn moist in wet season on account of its absorbent quality.

II

THE WHEEL OF FORTUNE

Mr. Gandhi during his visit to Assam and Eastern Bengal has observed, that the type of *charkha* in use in those parts is deficient in many ways. The same is perhaps the case in other provinces. As we believe that the *charkha* in the Satyagrahashram is a model of its kind, we give below a diagram with measurements of all its parts with an explanation of their relative functions.

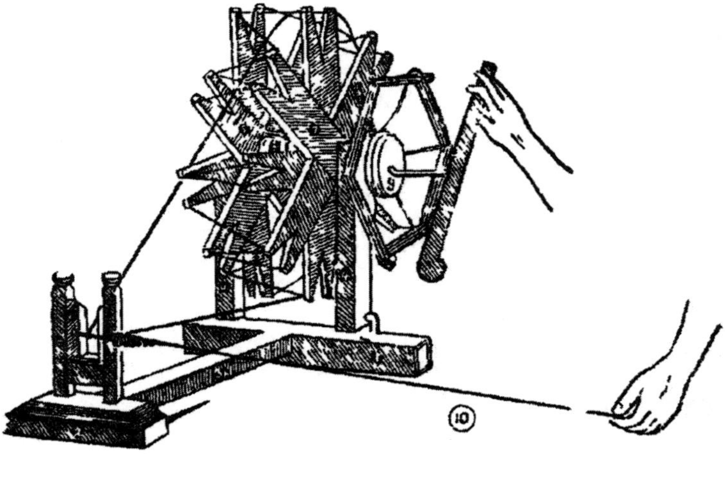

The rear base with mark *1* is one foot 9 inches long, 4inches wide and 3 inches high.

The front base with mark *2* is 9 inches long, 4 inches wide and 3 inches high.

The long piece which joins the two bases, marked *3*, is 3 feet long (including joints), 3 inches wide and 2 inches high.

The large uprights marked *4* are 1 foot 6 inches long including joints, 2 inches wide, and 3 inches deep. They are fixed on the back base 9 inches apart. The holes in which the axle rests are made 2 inches below the top. These holes contain bearings of thin iron plates to secure easy motion of the axle. The bearings are kept open at the top to allow access of oil through a slanting hole bored on the outward sides of both the uprights, one inch above the axle.

The small uprights marked *5* are 9 inches long with joints 1½ inches wide and 1½ inches deep, with holes 4 inches below the top to contain the leather bearings which bear the spindle. They are fixed 3 inches apart on the front base and are connected together 2 inches above the base with a piece of wood of the same thickness. This joining piece contains in the middle 2 sticks half an inch apart to regulate the position of the *mala* (the string which revolves the spindle) on the spindle.

Another piece marked *6* and joined parallelly to the left upright is meant to bear a hole for leather bearing when a thin spindle is to be used.

The drum or wheel consists of 8 planks such as the one marked *7*, each being 2 feet long, 4 inches wide and 3/4 inch thick. They are divided in two wings of 4 planks each, each containing two couples of planks joined diametrically with a groove in the middle.

Both the wings are nailed on to the wooden shaft marked *8*, its size being 4 ½ inches long and 4 inches diameter.

Through the middle of this shaft passes a long round iron bar, which serves as an axle. It is 19 inches long and half an inch thick. Its end where the handle is fixed is made square to ensure firmness of the handle.

A wooden washer one inch thick is fixed to the axle on either side of the drum to avoid its contact with the uprights.

The handle is shaped out of a wooden piece of 2 inches × 2 inches × 1 ½ feet long.

The reel noticed in the diagram between the drum and the handle is composed of a wooden disc marked *9* made out of 1 inch thick and 6 inches square piece of wood. Six brackets made of galvanized wire of 10 gauge radiate from the centre of the disc so as to make a circumference of 4 feet. The brackets are fixed in the back of the disc with bent ends and are further secured with small nails near the circumference of the disc.

A wire noose is fixed on the back base just below the reel to regulate the yarn when wound up on the reel from a bobbin or directly from the spindle.

A 4 inches long bamboo pin is fixed in the inward side of the front base parallelly to the long plank marked 3. It is meant to hold the bobbin while opening out yarn from it. When the yarn is opened from the spindle directly, it is held in the left hand with the point towards the reel. The right hand is employed in turning the reel by the handle of the *charkha.*

The figure *10*, indicates the position of the spinner.